Biblical Exploration
Natural Theology in Romans

Annabelle Knight

ABSTRACT

The Church's message to believers and unbelievers correctly emphasizes special revelation as essential for the Christian life. However, does this mean that natural theology and its use of general revelation have no relevance to the Church today? That is, should natural theology's use of what God reveals in nature independent of special revelation to reason Theism be ignored? This study summarizes from literature review natural theology's foundational concepts, including reason to pursue knowledge of the Christian worldview, its relationship to primary apologetic approaches, its major arguments, its historical use, and today's primary nontheistic worldviews. It also examines related Scripture passages, with focus on Romans 1:18-20's exposition of man's accountability to God due to natural revelation and thus his need for Christ's gospel. All to argue that natural theology, though incomplete for Christianity's communication without the special revelation of Christ's gospel, remains relevant to the Church especially in evangelism, impacting culture, and developing believers' relationship with God.

CONTENTS

CHAPTER 1: OVERVIEW OF THE STUDY 1
    Introduction 1
    Research Questions 2
    Problem Statement and Significance 3
    Thesis Statement 4
    Definition of Key Terms 4
    Research Plan 5
    Research Scope 7
    Structure 7

CHAPTER 2: LITERATURE REVIEW ON NATURAL THEOLOGY 9
    Pursuing Knowledge of Christian Worldview Truth through Reason and Faith 10
        Pursuing Knowledge of Truth that Affirms Reality 10
        Pursuing a Worldview of a Unified Set of Truths That Matter Most 12
        Pursuing Christian Worldview Truth through Reason and Faith 14
    Natural Theology Reasoning Used in Support of Apologetic Approaches 16
        Categorization of Major Christian Apologetic Approaches 18
        Approaches Emphasizing That Reason Can Lead toward Faith 20
        Approaches Emphasizing That Faith Is Necessary for True Reason 23
    Natural Theology's Major Arguments as Evidence for Theism 27
        Cosmological – From Universe's Finite Existence 30
        Design – From Universe's Designs for Life and Usefulness 32
        Ontological – From Human Idea of Perfect Being 35
        Moral – From Human Conscience's Knowing Moral Absolutes (Good/Evil) 36
        Other Arguments from Human Nature 38
    Natural Theology's Use during History 40
        Classical Greek and Roman Philosophy (500sBC-400sAD) 41
        Apostolic Age (30AD-300AD) 42
        Early Middle Ages (300AD-1000AD) 43
        Late Middle and Renaissance Ages (1000AD-1500AD) 44

  Reformation and Enlightenment Ages (1500AD-1800AD) 44

  Modern Age (1800AD-2000AD) 47

 Nontheistic Worldviews Today 48

  Modernism (Naturalism/Matterism) and Postmodernism 50

  Monism (Pantheism/Mindism) 55

CHAPTER 3: NATURAL THEOLOGY IN SCRIPTURE 58

 Natural Theology's Gospel Relevance in Romans 1:18-20: An Exegesis 59

  Place of Romans 1:18-20 Within Broader Context of Romans 60

  Structure and Main Motifs of Romans 1:18-20 and Surrounding Pericopes 63

  Romans 1:18-20 Detailed Exegesis 66

  Summary of Romans 1:18-20 Main Message and Objections 76

 Natural Theology's Apologetic Use by Paul in Acts 80

  Acts 14 Natural Theology 81

  Acts 17 Natural Theology 81

 Natural Theology's Relevance Exemplified in Other Scripture Passages 83

  Job's Natural Theology 83

  Through the Universe 85

  Through Human Nature 88

CHAPTER 4: NATURAL THEOLOGY'S RELEVANCE TODAY 92

 Natural Theology Use in Evangelism 94

  Being Personal, as in All Apologetics 95

  Finding Common Ground for Theistic Discussion 97

  Reasoning Theistic Truths in Contrast with Nontheistic Beliefs 98

 Natural Theology Use in Impacting Culture 101

  Impacting Collective Thought Toward Theism's Reasonability 101

  Impacting Cultural Spheres Toward Increased Truth/Good 102

 Natural Theology Use in Developing Believers' Relationship with God 106

  For Knowing God Better, Resolving Doubts, and Persevering 107

  For Confident Preparation for Evangelism and Impacting Culture 109

  For Scripture Interpretation 111

  Church Leadership Responsibility 114

CHAPTER 5: CONCLUSION 117

Summary of Research on Natural Theology's Place in the Church 117
    Literature Review Summary 117
    Scripture Research Summary 120
    Relevance to Church Ministries Today Summary 123

Final Recommendations on Natural Theology Use and Further Research 126
    Recommendations for Use Today 126
    Recommendations for Further Research 128

CHAPTER 1: OVERVIEW OF THE STUDY

Introduction

Do those hearing about Christianity already clearly understand who the Theistic God is from God's revelation through nature, and if not, should theistic truths be communicated to them along with the special revelation of Christ's gospel? The Church today does not seem to be clear or consistent about this. "Christianity does not begin with 'accept Christ as Savior,'" according to Francis Schaeffer, rather, "Christianity begins with 'In the beginning God created the heavens … and the earth.' That is the answer to the twentieth century and its lostness. … we are then ready to explain the second lostness (the original cause of all lostness) and the answer in the death of Christ."[1] Although Schaeffer wrote last century, it remains true today that "lostness" of a knowledge of the Theistic God can be an obstacle for many to considering Christ's gospel, especially when that gospel is presented without addressing their worldview's foundations. Further, that first "lostness" can be an obstacle to the culture being able to receive propositions of the Christian worldview and to believers' confidence when their worldview includes nontheistic concepts. Can/should the Church address that first "lostness" directly, and if so, should its communication include natural theology, which is the study and use of knowledge about the Theistic God reasoned from observed facts of nature apart from special revelation? That is, does natural theology have relevance today? This study presupposes that it does.

This chapter describes this study's research questions, states the problem being considered along with its significance, and specifies the thesis statement. Further, it defines key

---

1. Francis A. Schaeffer, *The Francis A. Schaeffer Trilogy* (Wheaton, IL: Crossway, 1990), 181.

terms and describes the research plan (including literature and Scripture review), its scope, and this study's organization.

Research Questions

This research topic was initiated following coursework in Christian apologetics which included natural theology. That coursework caused realization that seldom in my experience have I observed the Church communicating using philosophical arguments of natural theology. This includes in evangelism training, cultural interaction, and preaching/teaching.

The primary research question that results from the Church's seemingly limited use of natural theology without a sufficient explanation (at least in my experience) is this: Given the place that special revelation already has in the Church, does natural theology still have any relevance?

Many subordinate research questions arise on both what natural theology is and how it can/should be used. Key subordinate questions are:

Reason: Knowing that special revelation leading to faith responses to truth is essential for the Christian life, what role should reason (which is required for natural theology) play in the pursuit of knowledge of truth about God? How do faith and reason relate to general revelation and special revelation? Does reason help provide a common ground for believers with unbelievers?

Apologetic Approaches: What is natural theology as an apologetic approach? How does it support or contradict other approaches? What do proponents of its apologetic use argue for it? What do opponents of its use (who believe special revelation and faith are sufficient, and natural theology is ineffective or damaging to faith) argue against it?

Arguments: What are the major logical arguments used by natural theology? How, if at all, do they work together? For any one "argument," must it be stated in a specific way for effectiveness? Do the arguments relate to the basic life questions that people commonly have? Do the major natural theology arguments have specific relevance or a specific relationship with special revelation, and if so, what?

Church History: Has the Church used natural theology and its arguments throughout history? If so, how? That is, what was the purpose and the argument(s)?

Today's Worldviews: Do elements of today's prominent nontheistic worldviews make natural theology more or less relevant? Does culture ignore or argue against Theism? If so, how? Does a lack of using natural theology result in any challenges to people's knowledge of the truth of God?

Scripture: What does Paul say in a key passage related to this topic, Romans 1-3, especially 1:18-20? What do other related passages reveal?

Church Use Today: Should the Church use natural theology? If so, how? In evangelism, interacting with culture, and/or developing believers?

Problem Statement and Significance

Parts of the Church seem to ignore natural theology. Other parts believe special revelation is sufficient with no benefit from general revelation assisted by natural theology's theistic arguments, with some believing natural theology use is damaging. The primary problem being studied is this: can the Church's disregard or rejection of natural theology arguments have any negative consequences on its mission?

Whatever the cause of natural theology not being used, can various problems arise from these views with significant eternal consequences, depending on the circumstance? Concerning evangelism, if individual or group gospel communication does not address concepts foundational to a person's worldview, which natural theology theistic arguments may do, then can that person think of the gospel as unreasonable and fail to engage with and receive it? (It is acknowledged that other reasons may exist to cause persons to not receive the gospel.) Concerning connecting with culture, if an unbeliever does not accept minimally that Christianity is not simply a leap of faith but rather includes reasonable philosophical considerations, as natural theology theistic arguments promote, can that person be unable to accept theistic propositions (e.g., human endowment with inalienable right to life) being presented to the culture? Concerning a believer's confidence in the faith, if one's worldview contains some significant nontheistic beliefs, can that person be influenced by them to leave the faith unless natural theology's theistic arguments facilitate their replacement?

God through special revelation can overcome any of the above potential problems, but sometimes the reason of natural theology arguments causes persons to further consider Christianity and its propositions. I for one was drawn to seek God and commit to Christ after considering natural theology's truth and beauty arguments. In summary, they ask how can truth exist in its many forms (mathematical, scientific, etc.) without an eternal, rational, purposeful, all-powerful God creating it and how can beauty exist in its many forms (literature, art, persons, nature's scenes, etc.) without the same?

Thesis Statement

This study argues that although special revelation remains very essential for the Christian life, natural theology is equally relevant to the Church especially in evangelism, impacting culture, and developing believers' relationship with God.

Definition of Key Terms

This section provides definitions of key terms used within this study.

Apologetic – "a particular approach to the defense of the faith"[2]

Apologetics – "the discipline concerned with the defense of the faith", "a general grouping of approaches or systems developed for defending the faith", or "the practice of defending the faith"[3]

Classical Apologetics – "an apologetic approach that emphasizes the use of logical criteria ... in determining the validity of competing religious philosophies," which "in its modern form is characterized by a 'two-step' method of apologetics in

---

2. Kenneth D. Boa and Robert M. Bowman Jr., *Faith Has Its Reasons: Integrative Approaches to Defending the Christian Faith, 2nd Ed.* (Downers Grove, IL: InterVarsity Press, 2005), 4.

3. Ibid.

which one first makes a case for theism ... and then presents evidence that this God has revealed himself in Christ and in the Bible"[4]

General Revelation – "certain knowable truths about [the Theistic God]" that He has revealed in creation,[5] including in the universe and in human nature, generally to all humans

Natural Theology – "rational arguments for the existence of a monotheistic God that do not appeal to sacred scriptures for their cogency," but rather make use of general revelation[6]

Special Revelation – truths about the Christian God that He has revealed in Scripture[7]

Theism – religions that "[affirm] that there is only one God and that this God is a personal and Perfect Being of unlimited power, knowledge, and goodness who created the universe out of nothing. This being is worthy of adoration and worship, is distinct from the world but continuously involved in it, and is capable of generating miracles"[8]

Worldview – "'a comprehensive view of reality in terms of which one attempts to understand and "place" everything that comes before one's consciousness' ... an interrelated cluster of central assumptions or presuppositions about reality"[9]

Research Plan

The research plan involves scripture and literature (theological and historical) review related to the research topic's questions and problems, with analysis to identify major themes/issues and to clarify a thesis. Concerning scripture review, because the key scripture passage related to natural theology is Romans 1:18-20, Romans exposition materials are reviewed. Paul's Acts 14 and 17 apologetic encounters with gentiles are discussed by many

---

4. Ibid., 34.

5. Douglas Groothuis, *Christian Apologetics: A Comprehensive Case for Biblical Faith* (Downers Grove, IL: InterVarsity Press, 2011), 173-174.

6. Ibid., 171, 173-174.

7. Ibid., 180.

8. Ibid., 171.

9. Ibid., referencing Halverson, 74.

theologians relative to natural theology; therefore, materials on these are considered. Also, other relevant scripture passages are reviewed.

Concerning literature review, mainly literature of recent decades is reviewed, plus some older material containing unique content or considered classically important by more recent authors. Materials obtained initially include articles from the Regent University library databases on religion (natural theology from theological and historical perspectives) and apologetics overview books (with articles by many or written by one or two authors). Other materials include books/articles by authors referenced in initial materials or needed to answer open questions, including expanding to general Christian philosophy.

Analysis to identify major themes/issues and to clarify a thesis found that there exist differing opinions in these areas of investigation:

- differing views of reason's value relative to faith
- differing apologetic approaches, caused partially by theological views of faith and reason, with natural theology supporting one (classical apologetics) of four primary approaches
- differing natural theology arguments, with various proponents emphasizing different arguments, although some promote a cumulative approach integrating multiple arguments; for each argument, differing specifications of logic and conclusions on God's attributes derived from the argument
- differing emphases during Church historical use
- differing classifications/descriptions of today's nontheistic worldviews
- differing views on the meaning of Romans 1:18-20 and of Paul's gentile apologetic approaches

These will be discussed within this study. The first two and last are most significant, because they help determine whether one is a proponent of natural theology or not.

Research Scope

This study's thesis indicates that its focus is the relevance of using natural theology. Research attempts to adequately cover all major concepts of natural theology foundations (reason, apologetic approach, major arguments, historical use, current nontheistic worldviews) and of related Scripture. However, the scope does not permit exhaustive research into every viewpoint or objection of these aspects.

Because of this study's scope, the intended audience primarily includes Christians and especially Church leaders who might desire an introduction to natural theology and a discussion of its possible relevance for Church use. Secondarily, non-Christians might desire to better understand part of the Christian worldview through this portion of Christian reasoning (though there is much more). For both audiences, the hope is that some will research further, which can be started through this study's referenced works.

Structure

This study will begin by providing a literature review of natural theology's foundations then review what Scripture says on the subject before discussing how the Church can use natural theology today. Chapter 2's presentation from literature review summarizes natural theology's foundational concepts, including reason's use in pursuit of knowledge of Christian worldview truth, its use as part of apologetic approaches, and its major arguments. Chapter 2 further reviews natural theology's historical use and summarizes nontheistic worldviews. Chapter 3 provides a detailed exegesis of the main Scripture text, Romans 1:18-20, analyzing Paul's assertions concerning human knowledge of and suppression of general revelation and what those assertions suggest relative to natural theology's potential usage in gospel communication. Chapter 3 also examines other Scripture passages related to general revelation and natural theology, including

Acts on Paul's apologetics with gentiles, Job, and others. Chapter 4 focuses on the relevance of natural theology in today's Church, specifically in its ministries of evangelism, impacting culture, and developing believers' relationship with God. Chapter 5 offers a summary of findings and concluding recommendations.

Scripture quotations are from the New American Standard Bible 2020 (NASB2020) unless otherwise indicated.

CHAPTER 2: LITERATURE REVIEW ON NATURAL THEOLOGY

This chapter summarizes literature review on natural theology within a structure based on natural theology's foundational concepts as evident in the review. The concepts include: *reason* (the validity of pursuing Christian truth through not only faith but also reason based on reality), *apologetic approaches* (how natural theology reasoning fits within Christian apologetic approaches), *arguments* (its major arguments for Theism), *history* (how its arguments have been used during history), and *today's worldviews* (other primary worldviews that Theism defends against).

This study reviews material from the following types of works and authors:

- Edited volumes providing natural theology or general apologetics overviews, including by Sweis and Meister,[10] Holden,[11] Craig and Moreland,[12] and Re Manning.[13] Boa and Bowman's[14] overview volume summarizes many authors.

- Single author volumes providing classical apologetics overviews promoting their own arguments (including Groothuis,[15] Geisler,[16] and Craig)[17]

---

10. Khaldoun A. Sweis and Chad V. Meister, Eds., *Christian Apologetics: An Anthology of Primary Sources* (Grand Rapids, MI: Zondervan, 2012).

11. Joseph M. Holden, Ed., *The Comprehensive Guide to Apologetics* (Eugene, OR: Harvest House Publishers, 2018).

12. William Lane Craig and J. P. Moreland, Eds., *The Blackwell Companion to Natural Theology* (Chichester, West Sussex, UK: Wiley-Blackwell, 2012).

13. Russell Re Manning, Ed., *The Oxford Handbook of Natural Theology* (Oxford, U.K.: Oxford University Press, 2013).

14. Boa and Bowman, *Faith Has Its Reasons*.

15. Groothuis, *Christian Apologetics* (2011).

16. Norman L. Geisler, *Christian Apologetics, 2nd Ed.* (Grand Rapids, MI: Baker Academic, 2013).

17. William Lane Craig, *Reasonable Faith: Christian Truth and Apologetics, 3rd Ed.* (Wheaton, IL: Crossway, 2008).

- Single author volumes providing natural theology overviews promoting their own arguments (including Swinburne's two works).[18,19]

- Volumes and articles by various authors providing additional insight on a specific natural theology aspect, including philosophy or apologetics.

Pursuing Knowledge of Christian Worldview Truth through Reason and Faith

Natural theology provides reasoned arguments to promote knowledge of theistic worldview truths (that is, theistic truths of the Christian worldview). Literature review reveals many Christian authors of apologetics and philosophy including discussion of the foundation of pursuing knowledge of Christian worldview truth through reason and faith. Discussion here summarizes pursuing knowledge of truth that affirms reality, pursuing a worldview consisting of a unified set of truths that matter most, and pursuing Christian worldview truth through both reason and faith.

Pursuing Knowledge of Truth that Affirms Reality

Knowledge of truth, especially that which matters most, should be pursued and must affirm reality. Concerning pursuit, Pascal declares, "I should, therefore, like to arouse in man the desire to find truth ... realizing how far his knowledge is clouded."[20] Groothuis calls for being "ruthless with oneself in the process of pursuing truth, given the manifold temptations to self-deception and denial."[21] Acknowledging that objective truth is embattled, he asserts that

---

18. Richard Swinburne, *The Coherence of Theism, 2nd Ed.* (Oxford, UK: Oxford University Press, 2016).

19. Richard Swinburne, *The Existence of God, 2nd Ed.* (Oxford, UK: Oxford University Press, 2004).

20. Douglas R. Groothuis, "Why Truth Matters Most: An Apologetic for Truth-Seeking in Postmodern Times," *Journal of the Evangelical Theological Society* 47, no. 3 (September 2004), https://search-ebscohost-com.ezproxy.regent.edu/login.aspx?direct=true&db=rfh&AN=ATLA0001457915&site=ehost-live, 446.

21. Ibid., 443.

pursuing truth should not only be an aspiration, but a duty, because its enemies are great including sloth, apathy, and amusements.[22]

Concerning the need for truth to affirm reality, Christian authors agree. DeWeese and Moreland promote a correct theory of knowledge (epistemology, how I know what is real) saying, "most philosophers ... understand knowledge to be (approximately) *justified true belief*," with its belief as "an affirming or accepting mental state directed at an object – a proposition," its truth as "determined by a relation between [the] proposition and the world" according to the correspondence theory of truth, and its justification as the reason meeting a certain standard.[23] Moreland and Craig defend the correspondence theory, proclaiming:

> [it is] roughly, the idea that truth is a matter of a proposition (belief, thought, statement, representation) corresponding to reality ... called the classical theory of truth because ... it was held by virtually everyone until the nineteenth century. ... there is no particularly Christian theory of truth, one that is used only in the Bible and not elsewhere. ... truth does not vary from person to person ... **absolute truth**, also called **objective truth** ... people discover truth, they do not create it.[24]

Kelly and Dew call this theory "the common-sense ... mode."[25] Groothuis specifies eight features of a biblical view of truth, including: revealed by God, objectively existing/knowable, and absolute in nature.[26] Geisler asserts that a "Christian merely uses reason to *discover* truth that God has revealed, either by general revelation or by special revelation in the Bible."[27] Koukl

---

22. Groothuis, *Christian Apologetics* (2011), 16, 139-154.

23. Garrett J. DeWeese and J. P. Moreland, *Philosophy Made Slightly Less Difficult: A Beginner's Guide to Life's Big Questions, 2nd Ed.* (Downers Grove, IL: InterVarsity Press, 2021), 47-61.

24. J. P. Moreland and William Lane Craig, *Philosophical Foundations for a Christian Worldview, 2nd Ed.* (Downers Grove, IL: InterVarsity Press, 2017), 118-120.

25. Stewart E. Kelly and James K. Dew Jr., *Understanding Postmodernism: A Christian Perspective* (Downers Grove, IL: InterVarsity Press, 2017), 218.

26. Douglas Groothuis, *Truth Decay: Defending Christianity Against the Challenges of Postmodernism* (Downers Grove, IL: InterVarsity Press, 2000), 65-81.

27. Boa and Bowman, *Faith Has Its Reasons*, quoting Geisler, 72.

notes that when beliefs about reality "match up with the world ... we know our beliefs are true."[28] Howe also vigorously defends this theory.[29]

Pursuing a Worldview of a Unified Set of Truths That Matter Most

A worldview consists of a set of truths about that which matters most, a "broad-ranging theory of everything, in that it tries to account for the nature and meaning of the universe and its inhabitants."[30] A worldview should hold up to certain tests, both as individual truths and as a unified set. The truths of Christianity can be considered a worldview.

Describing what makes up a worldview, Schaeffer says one's system must answer the crucial questions about reality of existence, consisting of two primary parts: the universe exists and has a form and man is unique with qualities that must be explained.[31] Worldview answers "the most basic questions humans can face ... *the things that mean most to them*," Huntington observes.[32] Groothuis says it addresses "questions of hope, meaning, truth, morality and rationality,"[33] further explaining,

> A worldview ... is an overall conception of reality that touches on the key areas that philosophy and religion have always addressed ... 'a comprehensive view of reality in terms of which one attempts to understand and "place" everything that comes before one's consciousness' ... central assumptions or pre-suppositions about reality ... will typically include narrative elements as well ... the sense of an unfolding story of the cosmos and human history, and not just by a set of abstract statements.[34]

---

28. Gregory Koukl, *The Story of Reality: How the World Began, How It Ends, and Everything Important That Happens in Between* (Grand Rapids, MI: Zondervan, 2017), 31.

29. Richard G. Howe, "What Is Truth?," *The Comprehensive Guide to Apologetics*, Ed. Joseph M. Holden (Eugene, OR: Harvest House Publishers, 2018), 57, 59.

30. Groothuis, *Christian Apologetics* (2011), 49-50.

31. Schaeffer, *The Francis A. Schaeffer Trilogy*, 178.

32. Groothuis, *Christian Apologetics* (2011), quoting Huntington, 19.

33. Ibid., 19.

34. Ibid., 74.

Koukl observes "the basic parts of a good story actually match the basic parts of a worldview: beginning (creation), conflict (fall), conflict resolution (redemption), and ending (restoration)."[35]

Regarding tests for worldview truths individually and as a set, Geisler specifies that testing between worldviews must determine affirmability (adequately explaining, not self-defeating) and undeniability, whereas testing individual truths within a worldview must determine systematic coherence (consistency, empirical adequacy, and experiential relevance).[36] For worldview evaluation Groothuis describes eight criteria, each the same as or derived from criteria for evaluating any hypothesis.[37] He summarizes, worldview credibility "is determined by whether or not arguments marshaled in its favor are compelling and logically coherent."[38]

Christianity is considered a worldview, for it is "a large-scale hypothesis (or metanarrative) that attempts to explain what matters most" and "a system of truth claims or assertions about reality," according to Groothuis.[39] He notes that a Christian worldview consists not only of the outline of "the biblical drama of God, humanity and the cosmos" but also truths about God, humanity, salvation, ethical living, and God's rule (kingdom) on earth and in the afterlife.[40] Koukl asserts, *"Christianity is a picture of reality* ... not just a view from the inside [personal feelings/beliefs/affections/views] ... also a view of the outside ... how the world really is in itself ... beliefs about things like meaning, value, purpose, and significance.[41] Schaeffer

---

35. Koukl, *The Story of Reality*, 25, 27.

36. Geisler, *Christian Apologetics, 2nd Ed.*, 132-135.

37. Groothuis, *Christian Apologetics* (2011), 52-59.

38. Ibid., 50.

39. Ibid., 49, 75-76.

40. Ibid., 81-92.

41. Koukl, *The Story of Reality*, 23.

claims Christianity is a unity, "a whole system of truth ... the only system that will stand up to all the questions ... as we face the reality of existence," primarily related to the universe and human nature.[42]

Pursuing Christian Worldview Truth through Reason and Faith

Concerning pursuit of Christian worldview truth, Beilby wisely ponders, *"What is the relationship between faith and reason? Do we start with faith and only then try to explain it? Or is it possible to provide reasons for Christianity and only then, on the basis of those reasons, commit oneself in faith? There is ... a continuum of possible answers to this question."*[43] A latter section presents apologetic approaches promoting faith being requisite to reasoning; however, this section considers the more prevalent view that reason can have value prior to faith.

Reason has value in pursuing knowledge of truth, including Christian worldview truth. DePoe argues, "apologetics in all of its forms makes an appeal to people's autonomous reasoning. ... asking someone to change his mind about God based on reason. ... consider the doctrine of 'common grace' ... that God has blessed all humans with unmerited gifts regardless of their moral standing before Him. Among the gifts ... intellectual capacities."[44] Hanna agrees, saying, "reason is a God-given capacity to seek the truth and to acquire genuine knowledge."[45] "There is no reason to follow and obey the God of the Bible unless Christianity is true and worth obeying," proclaims Groothuis, "what the gospel requires of a person and on what basis it

---

42. Schaeffer, *The Francis A. Schaeffer Trilogy*, 178.

43. James K. Beilby, "Varieties of Apologetics," *Christian Apologetics: An Anthology of Primary Sources*, Eds. Khaldoun A. Sweis and Chad V. Meister (Grand Rapids, MI: Zondervan, 2012), 29.

44. John M. DePoe, "The Place of Autonomous Human Reason and Logic in Theology," *Without Excuse: Scripture, Reason, and Presuppositional Apologetics*, Ed. David Haines (Leesburg, VA: The Davenant Press, 2020), 61.

45. Mark M. Hanna, "What Is the Relationship Between Faith and Reason?," *The Comprehensive Guide to Apologetics*, Ed. Joseph M. Holder (Eugene, OR: Harvest House Publishers, 2018), 52-54.

requires it ... is classically known as *notitia*. One cannot be a Christian without knowing what Christianity actually is."[46] Geisler answers a key question by saying, "There is no contradiction between reason and evidence on one hand and the work of the Holy Spirit on the other."[47]

Faith also has value in pursuing Christian worldview truth, including when cooperating with reason. Moreland and Craig summarize the relationship:

> It is sometimes claimed that faith and reason are hostile to each other, and whatever is of reason cannot be of faith. But this represents a misunderstanding of the biblical concept of **faith**. ... Belief *in* rests on belief *that*. One is called to trust in what he or she has reason to give intellectual assent ... to. In Scripture, faith involves placing trust in what you have reason to believe is true. Faith is not a blind, irrational leap into the dark. So faith and reason cooperate on a biblical view of faith.[48]

Broocks specifies three key ingredients to faith as knowledge, assent, and a non-blind trust based on knowledge and evidence.[49] "All human beings have faith in a generic sense, for everyone trusts in others and believes a variety of things," asserts Hanna, adding, "the similarity between this generic faith and the unique faith referred to in Scripture is formal in that both involve a subjective state of believing and an object of that belief. The object of biblical faith is ... God and His revelation."[50] Plantinga proposes that while true Christian faith "isn't *merely* a cognitive activity ... it is also *at least* a cognitive activity. It ... involves *believing* something."[51] "Clearly,

---

46. Groothuis, *Christian Apologetics* (2011), 39-40.

47. Ed Hindson, "What Is the Holy Spirit's Role in Apologetics?," *The Comprehensive Guide to Apologetics*, Ed. Joseph M. Holden (Eugene, OR: Harvest House Publishers, 2018), quoting Geisler, 73.

48. Moreland and Craig, *Philosophical Foundations for a Christian Worldview, 2nd Ed.*, 20.

49. Rice Broocks, *God's Not Dead: Evidence for God in an Age of Uncertainty* (Nashville, TN: Thomas Nelson, 2013), 28-30.

50. Hanna, "What Is the Relationship Between Faith and Reason?," 53-54.

51. Alvin Plantinga, *Knowledge and Christian Belief* (Grand Rapids, MI: Wm. B. Eerdmans Publishing Co., 2015), 57-58.

faith in God is a matter of both the heart and mind," states Crain.[52] Hanna further supports reason/faith cooperation, saying, "Nowhere in the Bible is faith contrasted with reason; on the contrary, the Bible always implicitly or explicitly unites them. ... Faith is contrasted with sight ... with works [for salvation] ... with mere assent ... without some clear understanding of what one should believe, there can be no genuine faith."[53] Schaeffer also joins faith to reason, asserting,

> there are two concepts concerning faith. ... One idea of faith would be a blind leap in the dark ... in which you believe something with no reason (or no adequate reason) ... The other idea ... is that you are asked to believe something and bow before something on the basis of good and adequate reasons. ... The biblical concept of faith is very much the second.[54]

Natural Theology Reasoning Used in Support of Apologetic Approaches

Natural theology's reasoned arguments for Theism from God's general revelation are used commonly as key components of an apologetic approach called classical apologetics. Additionally, some natural theology arguments in less formal forms may support some other apologetic approaches. Rhodes asserts, "Apologetics uses reason in the defense of the faith. ... Every aspect of apologetics entails the use of reason."[55] Groothuis characterizes the discipline of apologetics (derived from the Greek *apologia*, meaning a defense) in this manner:

> [Apologetics is] the ancient and ongoing discipline of defending and advocating Christian Theism. ... Is the Christian worldview true and rational? Is it worth believing and living out? Within these questions resides the discipline of Christian apologetics. It offers

---

52. Natasha Crain, "Why Does God Seem 'Hidden'?," *The Comprehensive Guide to Apologetics,* Ed. Joseph M. Holden (Eugene, OR: Harvest House Publishers, 2018), 81-82.

53. Hanna, "What Is the Relationship Between Faith and Reason?," 52-53.

54. Schaeffer, *The Francis A. Schaeffer Trilogy*, 182.

55. Ron Rhodes, "Foreword," *The Comprehensive Guide to Apologetics*, Ed. Joseph M. Holden (Eugene, OR: Harvest House Publishers, 2018), 15.

answers based on rational arguments. ... Apologetics is linked to theology, philosophy and evangelism, but it is not reducible to any one of these disciplines.[56]

Literature review reveals some Christian apologetics authors presenting only their own apologetics approach, others describing all major approaches. Discussion herein of major apologetic approaches and their relationship to natural theology includes a summary of the approach categorization by authors describing all four major approaches, further consideration of two approaches which emphasize reason can lead toward faith, and further consideration of two approaches that emphasize faith is necessary before true reason about God. Classical apologetics with its subset natural theology fits within approaches emphasizing reason can lead toward faith.

Several apologetic approach types are not discussed in depth herein, including hybrid/combined, inescapable rationalist, and pragmatist. In practice, many apologists use a hybrid/combined set of features from multiple major approaches. This is possible when such apologists do not hold staunchly to certain major approach beliefs that preclude other approaches. While too many unique hybrid/combined approaches exist to summarize them all, mentioned herein are cases of natural theology argumentation being added to various major approaches. The inescapable rationalist approach is not considered because its approach to knowing truth based solely on reason (rationality using only the mind with logically inescapable arguments) does not consider faith and therefore is not a Christian view.[57] The pragmatist approach, which asserts truth is solely that which is experientially workable/livable, is also not considered as it does not consider faith and therefore is not a Christian view; although, elements

---

56. Groothuis, *Christian Apologetics* (2011), 20, 23, 27.

57. Geisler, *Christian Apologetics, 2nd Ed.*, 19, 123.

of livability exist in other approaches because "we must be able to live consistently with our theory," as Schaeffer indicates.[58]

Categorization of Major Christian Apologetic Approaches

Apologetics authors who present a set of major apologetic approaches (or systems/methodologies) include Boa and Bowman, House, Beilby, Geisler, and Groothuis. These authors have much in common in approach categorization; although, they differ slightly in approach names and content. Beilby asserts that differing major approaches exist because apologists have differing answers to fundamental or meta-apologetic questions, including: faith/reason relationship, extent humans understand God's nature, Holy Spirit's role, truth's nature, and apologetics' task.[59]

Several of these authors are fairly consistent in their categorizations of four major approaches, which herein are termed classical, evidentialist, presuppositionalist, and fideist. House categorizes using these terms.[60] Boa and Bowman provide extensive full volume analysis of the four, identifying them (with their basis/criteria) as classical (reason/rationalist), evidentialist (fact/empirical), reformed (revelation/authoritarian), and fideist (faith/intuitive); note their term reformed for presuppositionalist.[61] Beilby categorizes the four into three "strategies," whereby his evidentialist strategy includes the classical and historical (which is

---

58. Ibid., 90, 98.

59. Beilby, "Varieties of Apologetics," 29, 30.

60. H. Wayne House, "What Are Some Apologetic Approaches?," *The Comprehensive Guide to Apologetics*, Ed. Joseph M. Holden (Eugene, OR: Harvest House Publishers, 2018), 38-40.

61. Boa and Bowman, *Faith Has Its Reasons*, xviii, 36.

similar to the above evidentialist) approaches, his presuppositionalist strategy is the presuppositionalist approach, and his experientialist strategy is the fideist approach.[62]

Several other authors categorize slightly differently. Geisler categorizes several approaches similar to the four above, with his personal theistic apologetics approach being a version of the above classical, his evidentialist approach similar to the above evidentialist, his fideist similar to the above presuppositionalist/reformed, and his experientialist approach similar to the above fideist/experientialist.[63] Additionally, Geisler describes a variety of non-Christian truth approaches and worldviews.[64] Groothuis includes four major approaches similar to the above, including his personal cumulative-case approach being a version of the above classical.[65] Additionally, Groothuis describes a fifth major approach termed reformed epistemology (argued in recent decades by Plantinga, Wolterstorff, and Alston), which argues that "belief in God and the entire Christian worldview is one kind of belief that may be properly basic," meaning that the Christian God can be known without reason as a basic human capability.[66] Plantinga relies on Aquinas and Calvin for his basic belief argumentation;[67] although, he also argues many natural theology arguments in various works.[68] Reformed epistemology has features similar to other approaches, but will not be discussed further as it is not as prevalent in literature as the major four.

---

62. Beilby, "Varieties of Apologetics," 31-36.

63. Geisler, *Christian Apologetics, 2nd Ed.*, 268, 293, 72, 56, 35.

64. Ibid., 123, 137-138.

65. Groothuis, *Christian Apologetics* (2011), 60-70.

66. Ibid., 64-65.

67. Plantinga, *Knowledge and Christian Belief*, 30-31.

68. Jerry L. Walls and Trent Dougherty, "Introduction," *Two Dozen (or so) Arguments for God: The Plantinga Project*, Eds. Jerry L. Walls and Trent Dougherty (New York, NY: Oxford University Press, 2018), 1-5.

Approaches Emphasizing That Reason Can Lead toward Faith

Of the four major apologetic approaches, two emphasize that truth known through reason can lead toward faith: *classical* and *evidentialist*. The classical approach focuses on reasoning both for Theism from natural theology and for Christian Theism from historical evidence of special revelation, whereas evidentialist focuses on reasoning solely from historical evidence of special revelation. Many advocates of these approaches acknowledge that faith can occur without prior conscious reasoning about truth; however, each promotes reason as what commonly leads to faith. Further, their proponents believe that non-Christians can understand reason about God in spite of being sinners and that the Holy Spirit can assist in applying reason toward faith in the Christian gospel.[69] To this author, these approaches seem to more closely correlate with Arminian conditional election theology, whereby God took action to provide for salvation's possibility and humans choose to receive it, than with Calvinist theology.

The classical apologetics approach refers to some differing styles. Generally, it uses logical criteria to both "refute the truth claims of non-Christian worldviews and to establish the existence of God through theistic proofs," with the term classical indicating it being the dominant approach through church history.[70] Typically authors characterize the approach as consisting of two steps or parts, one using natural theology arguments (to be discussed in a latter section) to reason for Theism and one using Christianity's basic historical truths from special revelation (often the same truths as those argued by evidentialists) to reason Christianity is the most reasonable theistic worldview. Groothuis' cumulative-case method is a classical two-step

---

69. House, "What Are Some Apologetic Approaches?," 38, 40.

70. Boa and Bowman, *Faith Has Its Reasons*, 34, 49.

approach.[71] House's classical approach consists of three steps, first addressing worldview considerations, then natural theology (Theism and miracles), then evidence for Scripture historicity and resurrection.[72] Similarly, Deal and Holden's approach identifies three steps, whereby the first is the philosophical foundation (truth, logic, objective meaning, existence) which considers the unbeliever's worldview (Schaeffer's "pre-evangelism"), the second is the theological foundation (God [natural theology], miracles, evil), and the third is the evidential foundation (NT reliability, Jesus, resurrection).[73] Geisler's approach provides a 12 point summary of the whole argument for Christianity, with three being natural theology arguments.[74]

The classical approach has various strengths and weaknesses. Boa and Bowman summarize its strengths as affirming the universal applicability of reason for confirming/refuting beliefs, raising awareness of worldview importance, and recognizing common ground with non-Christians.[75] They highlight potential weaknesses as sometimes depending on natural theology arguments of debated validity, overestimating reason's adequacy as a truth criterion, and not addressing non-rational dimensions of knowledge and belief.[76]

Proponents of faith necessary for reason approaches differ with classical approach proponents in their perspective of "natural theology." Some say natural theology is misleading or even damaging because of sin's noetic effects on human rationalization. Williams claims,

---

71. Groothuis, *Christian Apologetics* (2011), 60-70.

72. House, "What Are Some Apologetic Approaches?," 38.

73. Don Deal and Joseph M. Holden, "What Is the Overall Apologetic Task?," *The Comprehensive Guide to Apologetics,* Ed. Joseph M. Holden (Eugene, OR: Harvest House Publishers, 2018), 43-46.

74. Geisler, *Christian Apologetics, 2nd Ed.*, 268, 293.

75. Boa and Bowman, *Faith Has Its Reasons*, 127-130.

76. Ibid., 130-135.

natural theology fails to recognize two basic things. First …a person's knowledge at best is disproportionate to the knowledge of God … man's knowledge capacity is insufficient to arrive at a full knowledge of God. Second, though there is a general revelation … it is so perverted through mankind's sinfulness that people's minds are futile and incapable of discerning what God is disclosing. … It is ultimately only the person who has faith who can cry out, "The heavens are telling the glory of God."[77]

Some, including McGrath, use the term "natural theology" differently to mean a theology of nature, that is, the study of God's self-revelation in nature that is known only through Christian special revelation.[78]

The evidentialist approach also refers to some differing styles, all "[seeking] to ground the Christian faith primarily on empirical and historically verifiable facts."[79] Evidentialist arguments do not include arguments for theism from nature; they include those for Christianity from the historicity of such things as the New Testament (or certain of its books), Christ's miracles, and/or Christ's resurrection.[80] Many define this approach narrowly, including only evidence from special revelation of Scripture and Christ. For example, Almodovar summarizes evidentialist topics as "Christianity … is the only way of salvation and founded on the fact of the birth, ministry, miracles, death, and resurrection given by the evangelists who were actual eyewitnesses."[81] Habermas focuses logic on Jesus' resurrection.[82] Others define this approach more broadly, with some "[recasting] arguments from other apologetic approaches as elements in

---

77. J. Rodman Williams, *Renewal Theology: God, the World, and Redemption,* Vol. 1 of *Renewal Theology* (Grand Rapids, MI: Zondervan, 1990), 36.

78. Peter Harrison, "What Is Natural Theology?: (And Should We Dispense with It?)," *Zygon* 57, no. 1 (March 2022), https://search-ebscohost-com.ezproxy.regent.edu/login.aspx?direct=true&db=rfh&AN=ATLAiG0V220331000834&site=ehost-live, 117.

79. Boa and Bowman, *Faith Has Its Reasons*, 34.

80. Beilby, "Varieties of Apologetics," 33.

81. Nancy A. Almodovar, *Reasons to Reason: Defending the Faith Is Good for Christians* (Resource Publications: Eugene, OR: 2021), 13.

82. Boa and Bowman, *Faith Has Its Reasons*, 194-197.

an overall evidential case for the truth of Christianity."[83] Geisler classifies evidentialist as the emphasis on evidence that is primarily historical but can include rational (overlapping with classical), archaeological, and experiential (changed lives).[84] He argues that an approach using only historical reasoning is insufficient to provide a complete worldview.[85] House differentiates between the evidential part of a classical approach and an evidential approach, saying classical imposes a deductive argument focus (from logical premises) vs. evidential imposes an inductive focus (visual/tangible).[86]

The evidentialist approach has various strengths and weaknesses. Boa and Bowman specify its strengths as recognizing probability not certainty in belief, appealing to ordinary ways of knowing, and stressing factual evidence.[87] They indicate its weaknesses as assuming the theistic worldview, using hidden metaphysical presuppositions of reality's nature, and underestimating the human factor (presuppositional framework and potential noetic sin effects).[88]

Approaches Emphasizing That Faith Is Necessary for True Reason

Of the four major apologetic approaches, two emphasize that faith is necessary for true reason about God: *presuppositionalist/reformed* and *fideist/experientialist*. (Geisler uses the term fideist for what others term presuppositionalist/reformed; herein his terminology is not used.)

---

83. Ibid., 153.

84. Norman L. Geisler, *The Big Book of Christian Apologetics: An A to Z Guide* (Grand Rapids, MI: Baker Books, 2012), 29-30.

85. Geisler, *Christian Apologetics, 2nd Ed.*, 88.

86. House, "What Are Some Apologetic Approaches?," 39.

87. Boa and Bowman, *Faith Has Its Reasons*, 211-214.

88. Ibid., 214-217.

While both approaches emphasize special revelation, the presuppositionalist/reformed approach focuses on faith from special revelation in Scripture before true reasoning occurs, whereas fideist/experientialist focuses on faith experienced before true reasoning occurs. To this author, these approaches seem to more closely correlate with Calvinist unconditional election theology, whereby God takes action to cause salvation for the elect, than with Arminian theology.

The presuppositionalist approach consists of a well-defined style. Well-known presuppositionalist Val Til explains, "The Reformed apologist assumes that nothing can be known by man about himself or the universe unless God exists and Christianity is true," which means "any knowledge at all depends on knowledge of God and Christianity. ... Thus the revelation of God, the Christian Bible, is the first principle for 'Christian' ... knowledge."[89] For presuppositionalists, Christians must reason from a presupposed Christian worldview, and non-Christians cannot reason adequately about God.[90] Boa and Bowman indicate that presuppositionalists commonly reject the inductive and deductive apologetic reasoning used by classical and evidentialist approaches, arguing that by "[seeking] to use a method that non-Christians can accept, [those approaches] are actually seeking a method that assumes man's self-sufficiency."[91] Dennison characterizes Van Til as believing "the Bible presupposes that no one can interpret or understand the theistic construction of the creation unless one stands in the palm of the triune God of Scripture."[92] Further, Shannon reports that Van Til and Junius "agree that

---

89. M. Dan Kemp, "The Bible, Verification, and First Principles of Reason," *Without Excuse: Scripture, Reason, and Presuppositional Apologetics*, Ed. David Haines (Leesburg, VA: The Davenant Press, 2020), 3.

90. Groothuis, *Christian Apologetics* (2011), 62-64.

91. Boa and Bowman, *Faith Has Its Reasons*, 260.

92. William D. Dennison, "Natural and Special Revelation: A Reassessment," *Kerux* 21, no. 2 (September 2006), https://search-ebscohost-com.ezproxy.regent.edu/login.aspx?direct=true&db=rfh&AN=ATLA0001559759&site=ehost-live, 17.

post-fall natural theology, unaided by special revelation, is not theology in any meaningful sense. … since true theology is determined by redemptive relation."[93]

However, some presuppositionalists do not totally reject reason from nature, as they sometimes use it within argument forms similar to but more informal than those of formal natural theology. Frame (who identifies as presuppositionalist) uses arguments similar to natural theology but with Scripture passages supporting each, because "natural revelation does have a high importance, even in the salvation of sinners. … nature … serves as [the gospel's] presupposition, its foundation. And it establishes the reality of sin, which makes the gospel necessary."[94] Schaeffer, who declares "knowledge precedes faith … *faith which believes God on the basis of knowledge is true faith*," is sometimes portrayed as presuppositionalist and yet makes informal natural theology arguments as part of what he calls "pre-evangelism," which helps unbelievers understand their worldview and its logical end.[95] Thus, approaches like Frame's and Schaeffer's, though each apologist might be considered presuppositionalist, seem to validate at least informal natural theology argumentation as part of a complete apologetic for evangelism.

The presuppositionalist approach has various strengths and weaknesses. Its strengths as identified by Boa and Bowman include linking of apologetics and theology, raising epistemological consciousness, and challenging unbelief directly with its transcendental

---

93. Nathan D. Shannon, "Junius and Van Til on Natural Knowledge of God," *The Westminster Theological Journal* 82, no. 2 (Fall 2020), https://search-ebscohost-com.ezproxy.regent.edu/login.aspx?direct=true&db=rfh&AN=ATLAiA14210111000279&site=ehost-live, 279.

94. John M. Frame, *Nature's Case for God: A Brief Biblical Argument* (Bellingham, WA: Lexham Press, 2018), 3, 11.

95. Schaeffer, *The Francis A. Schaeffer Trilogy*, 154, 155, 178.

argumentation.[96] They summarize weaknesses as assuming a "rigidly dogmatic Calvinism," underestimating the power of facts, and limiting apologists to restrictive, abstract arguments.[97] This limiting leaves no common ground between believers and unbelievers, because unbelievers reasoning about God is ineffective due to the fall.[98] DePoe states, "presuppositionalists commonly reject the use of autonomous human reasoning" to consider what to believe about God.[99] Objections include that it makes arguments for the trustworthiness of Scripture circular and Scripture does not identify itself as the sole source of all knowledge.[100]

The fideist approach also consists commonly of a fairly well-defined style. The fideist's Christian truth "is fundamentally not some body of knowledge, but Somebody to know ... the truth is ultimately a person, Jesus Christ ... Kierkegaard ... insists that [reasons] will be unusable once [an unbeliever] has made the personal commitment of faith. In fact, he will not or should not use them even to help other unbelievers make the same commitment."[101] Further, to fideists, certain "basic, essential truths of the Christian message show us that God, as the object of our faith, is beyond understanding and beyond proof."[102] Fideists view Christianity as above reason so reason is ineffective.[103]

---

96. Boa and Bowman, *Faith Has Its Reasons*, 327-329.

97. Ibid., 329-333.

98. House, "What Are Some Apologetic Approaches?," 40.

99. DePoe, "The Place of Autonomous Human Reason and Logic in Theology," 56.

100. Kemp, "The Bible, Verification, and First Principles of Reason," 2, 29.

101. Boa and Bowman, *Faith Has Its Reasons*, 366-367.

102. Ibid., 368.

103. House, "What Are Some Apologetic Approaches?," 40.

The fideist approach also has various strengths and weaknesses. Strengths include emphasizing faith's personal dimensions over intellectual, viewing human knowledge/reason humbly, and centering on Christ.[104] But it has serious weaknesses, including undervaluing propositional knowledge about God, overstating criticisms of knowledge/reason, and undermining Scripture confidence by an unnecessarily negative view.[105] Groothuis declares that fideism ("faith-ism") disparages logic, proclaiming "faith means believing something without or against evidence and logic."[106] For fideists, not only is faith sufficient, but reason is harmful.[107]

Natural Theology's Major Arguments as Evidence for Theism

Natural theology provides arguments for Theism that are commonly categorized into multiple major categories. This section discusses the following four major argument categories: *cosmological* (from universe's finite existence), *design* (i.e., teleological, from universe's designs for life and usefulness), *ontological* (from human idea of perfect being), and *moral* (from human conscience's knowing moral absolutes). Additionally, a set of "other" arguments are summarized, all from human nature and none within the above four categories. Some authors use the term *anthropological* arguments for arguments from human nature, including moral arguments[108] and this study's "other" arguments; other authors use the term *psychological* arguments for those from human nature and cosmological for those noted above as cosmological

---

104. Boa and Bowman, *Faith Has Its Reasons*, 419.

105. Ibid., 420-422.

106. Groothuis, *Christian Apologetics* (2011), 45.

107. Ibid., 60-62.

108. Boa and Bowman, *Faith Has Its Reasons*, 97.

and design (ignoring ontological).[109] Those using natural theology believe it only provides theistic conclusions and that Christianity's special revelation truths are required to answer remaining life questions including evil/sin's resolution.[110] However, while all natural theology authors conclude Theistic God's existence, relatively few (excepting moral argument authors) clearly document the important corollary that man is accountable to God.

Various authors identify the set of valuable major arguments slightly differently. DeWeese and Moreland discuss the four noted above and add the religious experience argument and several minor others.[111] Craig explains those four major arguments, with much supporting detail for the first two from science.[112] Howe excludes ontological but includes the other three.[113] Groothuis describes not only the major four but adds those from religious experience and from human uniqueness (from mind's consciousness and reason and from greatness/sin, related to moral).[114] Deal and Holden identify major arguments as cosmological, teleological, moral, motion (from universe motion, related to cosmological), and anthropological (from intelligent beings).[115] Sweis and Meister include articles on the four major plus transcendental, religious experience, and human mind arguments.[116]

---

109. Peter Kreeft and Ronald K. Tacelli, *Handbook of Christian Apologetics: Hundreds of Answers to Crucial Questions* (Downers Grove, IL: Intervarsity Press, 1994), 49.

110. John H. Gerstner, *Reasons for Faith* (Coppell, TX: CrossReach Publications, 2016), 28-30.

111. DeWeese and Moreland, *Philosophy Made Slightly Less Difficult*, 180-192.

112. Craig, *Reasonable Faith*, 95-196.

113. Richard G. Howe, "What Are the Classical Proofs for God's Existence?," *The Comprehensive Guide to Apologetics*, Ed. Joseph M. Holden (Eugene, OR: Harvest House Publishers, 2018), 83.

114. Groothuis, *Christian Apologetics* (2011), 21.

115. Deal and Holden, "What Is the Overall Apologetic Task?," 45.

116. Sweis and Meister, Eds., *Christian Apologetics: An Anthology of Primary Sources*, 7-8.

Some authors combine multiple major arguments into a cumulative case argument.[117] Rasmussen uses all four major argument types plus mind arguments (consciousness and reason) within his very philosophical cumulative case.[118] Strobel combines cosmological, design, and consciousness/mind arguments, emphasizing multiple sciences support, in concluding God as intelligent designer.[119] Interestingly, in one volume Swinburne defends theism's internal coherence with logic building from God's initial attribute as omnipresent Spirit to other attributes;[120] while in another volume he describes three major arguments (excepting ontological) plus others including from consciousness, providence, and religious experience.[121] Craig uses all four major arguments, recommending a cumulative case because the variety "not only reinforces common conclusions but also rounds out the nature of [God]."[122]

Concerning natural theology argument proof certainty, DeWeese and Moreland claim "we do not think that God's existence can be 'proved' ... in the same sense that a mathematical or logical proof yields certainty. But the arguments for God's existence that have been offered through the centuries are, we think, able to establish the existence of God ... by a preponderance of the evidence, if not beyond a reasonable doubt."[123] Craig asserts that good apologetic arguments have greater plausibility than their denials, not 100% certainty, because certainty is

---

117. DeWeese and Moreland, *Philosophy Made Slightly Less Difficult*, 191.

118. Joshua Rasmussen, *How Reason Can Lead to God: A Philosopher's Bridge to Faith* (Downers Grove, IL: InterVarsity Press, 2019), vii.

119. Lee Strobel, *The Case for a Creator: A Journalist Investigates Scientific Evidence that Points Toward God* (Grand Rapids, MI: Zondervan, 2004), 300-301.

120. Swinburne, *The Coherence of Theism,* ix, 1.

121. Swinburne, *The Existence of God,* vii, 1.

122. Craig, *Reasonable Faith*, 190.

123. DeWeese and Moreland, *Philosophy Made Slightly Less Difficult*, 180.

unattainable and we do not obtain it in almost anything that we infer, adding we should simply claim, "in light of the evidence it's more probable than not that God exists."[124]

Levels of argument scope and formality differ between apologists using natural theology. Arguments consist of premises/propositions derived from God's general revelation in nature (universe and human nature) and conclusions that the Theistic God exists. Premises are best when appealing "to facts [of experience] which are widely accepted or to intuitions that are commonly shared (common sense)" and conclusions should use the laws of logic (another common ground with unbelievers).[125] Conclusions also sometimes specify God's attributes, and less often specify humanity's relationship to God; other times the attributes and relationship are assumed. For some authors the argument scope is quite extensive, to include not only supporting perspectives but also major objection rebuttals, benefitting the more academic audience; for others the scope is less detailed, though commonly sufficient, benefitting the less academic audience. For many authors the argument reasoning includes the formality of clearly identified premise and conclusion sentences with precise logic; whereas for others the reasoning is less formal, though understandable within descriptive text.

Cosmological – From Universe's Finite Existence

A cosmological argument contends that proper reasoning about the facts of the universe's (cosmos') existence generates the conclusion that the Theistic God exists and pre-existed and created it.[126] Swinburne emphasizes the complex physical universe's finiteness (compared to God's infiniteness) when he says a cosmological argument "starts from the existence of a finite

---

124. Craig, *Reasonable Faith*, 55, 189.

125. Ibid., 56-57.

126. Groothuis, *Christian Apologetics* (2011), 210.

object – that is, an object of limited power, knowledge, or freedom."[127] Schaeffer asserts, "The Christian presupposition is that there was a personal beginning to all things – someone has been there and made all the rest. ... the personal-infinite someone," with the alternative presupposition being an impersonal beginning and our current condition occurring through time and chance.[128] Much science, such as Laws of Thermodynamics and the Big Bang Theory, supports the idea of initial universe creation from nothing into finite time and physical (space with matter/energy) dimensions.[129]

Cosmological arguments are sometimes categorized under three main types, each starting with the universe's (or a human's) existence which therefore began and has a First Cause. Craig identifies the focus of the three types as: (1) Kalam forms, whereby prior to the universe's beginning in time there is an eternal First Cause; (2) Thomistic forms, whereby prior to the universe's causation(s) there is an all-powerful First Cause; and (3) Leibnizian forms, whereby prior to the universe's existence there is an all-knowing/reasoning First Cause to answer "why does it exist?"[130] Leibniz argues that humans have knowledge of necessary and eternal truths; reasoned truths each resolve to more simple truths/ideas until we come to those which are primary; and the final primary reason must be a necessary, infinite, perfect, supreme, Sufficient Reason/Being, from whom all other beings are contingent.[131] The cosmological underpinnings (which seem Leibnizian) of Rasmussen's argument assert that the blob of everything has a

---

127. Swinburne, *The Existence of God*, 133.

128. Schaeffer, *The Francis A. Schaeffer Trilogy*, 343.

129. Howe, "What Are the Classical Proofs for God's Existence?, 84.

130. Craig, *Reasonable Faith*, 96-99.

131. Gottfried Wilhelm Leibniz, "The Argument from Sufficient Reason," *Christian Apologetics: An Anthology of Primary Sources*, Eds. Khaldoun A. Sweis and Chad V. Meister (Grand Rapids, MI: Zondervan, 2012), 94-95.

"foundation" within it of independent nature (so blob is self-sufficient), of necessary existence (for independence), and of ultimacy (accounting for existence of anything); therefore, only the Theistic God can be that foundation.[132] Thomas Aquinas' Five Ways include primarily cosmological arguments, of which Baker describes three (Unmoved Mover, Necessary Being, and Perfect Being).[133] Geisler claims that the six self-evident first principles of reality (or being/existence) can be used to argue for Theism, with his ten step argument relying on the impossibility of infinite regression of cause (a Thomistic form).[134] Others believe similarly on cause regression, including Muller discussing Hale who says "there cannot be an infinity of actual things" and an infinite actual sequence is impossible.[135] Deal and Holden identify two versions of cosmological arguments, both primarily Thomistic (First Cause and First Mover).[136] Feser describes four cosmological arguments (from change, parts, existing things, and contingent things).[137]

Design – From Universe's Designs for Life and Usefulness

A design (also called teleological) argument contends that proper reasoning about the design of the universe (cosmos) generates the conclusion that the Theistic God exists and pre-existed and not only created but designed (purposed) it for life's existence and for usefulness.[138]

---

132. Rasmussen, *How Reason Can Lead to God*, 41.

133. Thomas W. Baker, "What Are Some Other Arguments for God's Existence?", *The Comprehensive Guide to Apologetics*, Ed. Joseph M. Holden (Eugene, OR: Harvest House Publishers, 2018), 89-94.

134. Geisler, *Christian Apologetics, 2nd Ed.*, 265-268.

135. Richard A. Muller, "Sir Matthew Hale on the Nature of Knowledge and the Relation of Natural to Supernatural Theology," *Mid-America Journal of Theology* 30 (2019), 64, https://search-ebscohost-com.ezproxy.regent.edu/login.aspx?direct=true&db=rfh&AN=ATLAiACO200622000077&site=ehost-live.

136. Deal and Holden, "What Is the Overall Apologetic Task?," 45.

137. Edward Feser, *Five Proofs of the Existence of God* (San Francisco, CA: Ignatius Press, 2017), 5.

138. Groothuis, *Christian Apologetics* (2011), 40.

Although the terms teleological and design are sometimes used interchangeably, often arguments emphasizing the end purpose/goal (often traditional arguments) are termed teleological while those emphasizing the design process (often scientific) are termed design. Howe says traditional design arguments propose that "because all things aim toward their destiny ... unless hampered by an external impediment, there must be someone who is directing things to their telos" (goal or purpose), an intelligence called God.[139] The term Intelligent Design (ID) expresses that pre-existent intelligence most probably produced what we observe.

Arguments from universal abstracts/laws can be considered design arguments. Feser describes an Augustinian argument in which the existence of unchanging, abstract, immaterial objects (such as numbers, mathematical concepts/laws, scientific laws/constants) advocates for an Intelligent Designer.[140] In an article titled as a transcendental argument Bahnsen argues that laws of nature and abstract universals, including those of logic and science, cannot be explained reasonably by nontheistic views including naturalism; therefore, Theism is most probable.[141]

Scientific findings at human, macro, and micro levels in recent centuries have initiated many more design arguments. In creating the 1802 classic volume of teleological arguments, Craig says "Paley combed the sciences of his day for evidences of design in nature and produced a staggering catalogue of such evidences, based, for example, on the order evident in bones, muscles, blood vessels, comparative anatomy, and particular organs throughout the animal and plant kingdoms."[142] Paley's famous watchmaker analogy asserts that just as the complex,

---

139. Howe, "What Are the Classical Proofs for God's Existence?," 85.

140. Feser, *Five Proofs of the Existence of God*, 106.

141. Greg Bahnsen and Gordon Stein, "A Transcendental Argument for God's Existence," *Christian Apologetics: An Anthology of Primary Sources*, Eds. Khaldoun A. Sweis and Chad V. Meister (Grand Rapids, MI: Zondervan, 2012), 161.

142. Craig, *Reasonable Faith*, 101.

purposeful order of a watch causes one to conclude its watchmaker exists and designed it, similarly the complex, purposeful order of the universe and life forms should cause one to conclude their Maker exists and designed them.[143] Enfield's 1821 classic also describes many inexplicable designs in nature on earth, all pointing to God's being, power, and goodness.[144]

More recent scientific discoveries such as universe/earth "fine-tuning" to support life continue to initiate design arguments. Many, including DeWeese and Moreland,[145] discuss fine-tuning arguments, which propose that the significant number of cosmological constants that have to be fine-tuned within small ranges for a universe and planet to support life and/or the smallness of the ranges required for life advocate that these conditions most probably are caused by intelligence. Collins emphasizes the validity of probability calculus when judging fine-tuning reasonability, with the argument (extraordinary balancing of cosmos' physics parameters and initial conditions) being not improbable under Theism but very improbable under atheism.[146]

Additional discoveries initiating design arguments include "irreducible complexity" findings in many macro, human, and micro systems. Behe defines irreducible complexity as existence of a system "composed of several interacting parts, and where the removal of any one of the parts causes the system to cease functioning."[147] Behe asserts that this major observation

---

143. William Paley, *Natural Theology* (New York, NY: Oxford University Press, 2008), Reprint from 1802, 7-15.

144. William Enfield, M.A. *Natural Theology: Or, a Demonstration of the Being and Attributes of God, From His Works of Creation: Arranged in a Popular Way for Youth* (Publication city not documented: Nabu Press, 2012), ISBN-13 978-1272537722, A Nabu Public Domain Reprint of book (Hartford, CT: G. Goodwin and Sons, 1821), 2-6.

145. DeWeese and Moreland, *Philosophy Made Slightly Less Difficult*, 187.

146. Robin Collins, "A Recent Fine-Tuning Design Argument," *Christian Apologetics: An Anthology of Primary Sources*, Eds. Khaldoun A. Sweis and Chad V. Meister (Grand Rapids, MI: Zondervan, 2012), 106, 109.

147. Michael J. Behe, "Evidence for Intelligent Design from Biochemistry," *Christian Apologetics: An Anthology of Primary Sources*, Eds. Khaldoun A. Sweis and Chad V. Meister (Grand Rapids, MI: Zondervan, 2012), 101.

in various sciences including biochemistry (e.g., operation of vision, cilia, and blood clotting) points to Intelligent Design rather than Darwin's simplistic evolution and that as complexity increases confidence in Darwin's indirect route of creation decreases dramatically.[148] Another biochemistry argument noted by DeWeese and Moreland (and others) advocates intelligent design based on every organism's genome (DNA) containing vast amounts of information.[149]

Ontological – From Human Idea of Perfect Being

An ontological argument contends that "proper reasoning about the idea of a Perfect Being generates the conclusion that [the Theistic God] exists."[150] Anselm in 1078 records ontological arguments, including that God is a being than which nothing greater can be conceived and has a necessary existence (based on logical modality); however, his reasoning has encountered serious objections.[151] Plantinga provides an updated argument based on metaphysical modality in which he identifies his argument's central premise as the existence of a maximally great being with omniscience, omnipotence, and moral perfection in every possible world, concluding that his argument does not establish Theism's truth but its "rational acceptability."[152] Plantinga's argument "seems free from any clear logical errors," according to DeWeese and Moreland, but "is not especially easy to understand, and so it is not rationally compelling for most people."[153]

---

148. Ibid., 99-105.

149. DeWeese and Moreland, *Philosophy Made Slightly Less Difficult*, 187.

150. Groothuis, *Christian Apologetics* (2011), 185.

151. DeWeese and Moreland, *Philosophy Made Slightly Less Difficult*, 180-184.

152. Alvin Plantinga, "A Recent Modal Ontological Argument," *Christian Apologetics: An Anthology of Primary Sources*, Eds. Khaldoun A. Sweis and Chad V. Meister (Grand Rapids, MI: Zondervan, 2012), 136-138.

153. DeWeese and Moreland, *Philosophy Made Slightly Less Difficult*, 184.

Many authors do not describe ontological arguments, possibly because they can be difficult for the non-philosophical person to understand or because argument logic is not trusted. Boa and Bowman declare that only the ontological reasons "in a purely *a priori* fashion (derived from certain assumptions or ideas as given)."[154] Maydole, after providing a highly technical exposition of many ontological arguments including Anselm's, Plantinga's, and others, concludes that "some ontological arguments are sound, do not beg the question, and are insulated from extant parodies" and even so sometimes they do not convince.[155]

Moral – From Human Conscience's Knowing Moral Absolutes (Good/Evil)

A moral argument contends that proper reasoning about human conscience's knowledge of objective moral reality generates the conclusion that the Theistic God exists and is the moral creator and revealer of that reality.[156] Some classify such arguments as axiological (study of value/goodness).[157] Others categorize them as ethical (emphasizing behavior).[158]

Many refer to a divine, universal Moral Lawgiver as the best explanation for the truth of certain human moral judgments from innate moral law. In Baggett and Walls' moral argument volume, they review historical moral argument versions to identify best insights such as Moral Lawgiver (divine commands), moral freedom (required based on God's love), and moral authority/obligation (values of goodness, actions of rightness).[159] Deal and Holden are amongst

---

154. Boa and Bowman, *Faith Has Its Reasons*, 98.

155. Robert E. Maydole, "The Ontological Argument," *The Blackwell Companion to Natural Theology*, Eds. William Lane Craig and J. P. Moreland (Chichester, West Sussex, UK: Wiley-Blackwell, 2012), 586.

156. Groothuis, *Christian Apologetics* (2011), 332.

157. Moreland and Craig, *Philosophical Foundations for a Christian Worldview, 2nd Ed.*, 500.

158. Geerhardus Vos, *Natural Theology* (Grand Rapids, MI: Reformation Heritage Books, 2022), a translation of late nineteenth century lectures, 67.

159. David Baggett and Jerry L. Walls, *The Theistic Foundations of Morality* (New York, NY: Oxford University Press, 2011), 7-29, 31-48, 65-89, 103-123.

others using the Moral Lawgiver term.[160] Moral argument authors sometimes address the problem of evil (necessary from free will) within the argument, and sometimes in lengthy supporting material.

Authors propose slightly differing views on the universality of a singular moral code. C. S. Lewis argues that everyone assumes the law of human nature, believing everyone else was created with innate respect for human value and therefore lives a certain level of decent behavior.[161] Lewis' moral argument version concludes that "only an infinite personal source can explain universal morality."[162] DeWeese and Moreland opine, "moral arguments do not necessarily presuppose a common morality or a universal moral code ... Rather, they recognize that there is among humans [excluding sociopaths] a common moral consciousness, a universal tendency to make moral judgments."[163] In a moral argument volume by Haines and Fulford, they examine "natural law," defined as the human conduct rule based on created human nature, knowable by all without special revelation, and normative for all.[164] Rasmussen proposes our "moral senses are a *window* into a moral landscape" provided by the Moral Foundation, whereby that moral window "provides *some* sight to *some* extent."[165]

Some authors defend their moral argument against naturalism. Copan's thorough moral argument explains that "a moral universe and human dignity are best explained in the context of

---

160. Deal and Holden, "What Is the Overall Apologetic Task?," 45.

161. C. S. Lewis, "God and the Moral Law," *Christian Apologetics: An Anthology of Primary Sources*, Eds. Khaldoun A. Sweis and Chad V. Meister (Grand Rapids, MI: Zondervan, 2012), 171-173.

162. DeWeese and Moreland, *Philosophy Made Slightly Less Difficult*, 188.

163. Ibid.

164. David Haines and Andrew A. Fulford, *Natural Law: A Brief Introduction and Biblical Defense* (Lincoln, NE: The Davenant Press, 2017), 5.

165. Rasmussen, *How Reason Can Lead to God*, 110.

a morally excellent, worship-worthy Being as their metaphysical foundation, as opposed to nontheistic alternatives, and naturalism in particular," and further that arguments against Theism from the existence of evil assume a fundamental standard of goodness (and human value) which is unreasonable without Theism.[166] Copan's direct defense against Hume's naturalism asserts that "the moral argument does not purport to show that the ultimate standard of goodness is necessarily all-powerful and all-wise, but it is sufficient to render us morally accountable to a personal Being in whose image we have been made."[167]

Human pricelessness is correctly emphasized by some authors. In Baggett and Baggett's moral argument volume, a human's sense of priceless personal value/worth/dignity comes from being made in God's image and sense of moral obligation comes from God's loving revelation through conscience of how to best live.[168] Linville says moral argument conclusions mean moral obligation is "owed" from human to human because all are pricelessly created as persons, a feature of their creator God.[169]

Other Arguments from Human Nature

Arguments other than the four major arguments above exist that propose proper reasoning about some aspect of human nature concludes theism's God exists. These human nature aspects are all of the spirit/soul, not of the body. The existence and greatness of these aspects do not seem reasonable based on naturalism's (physicalism's) proposed accidental

---

166. Paul Copan, "The Moral Argument," *Christian Apologetics: An Anthology of Primary Sources*, Eds. Khaldoun A. Sweis and Chad V. Meister (Grand Rapids, MI: Zondervan, 2012), 174-176.

167. Paul Copan, "Hume and the Moral Argument," *In Defense of Natural Theology: A Post-Humean Assessment*, Eds. James F. Sennett and Douglas Groothuis (Downers Grove, IL: InterVarsity Press, 2005), 201-202.

168. David Baggett and Marybeth Baggett, *The Morals of the Story: Good News About a Good God* (Downers Grove, IL: InterVarsity Press, 2018), 219-229.

169. Mark D. Linville, "Moral Particularism," *God and Morality: Four Views*, Ed. R. Keith Loftin (Chichester, West Sussex, UK: Wiley-Blackwell, 2012), 158.

creation of them from nothing or from matter, but do seem reasonable based on Theism's purposeful creation by a personal, all-powerful, spirit Being.

Authors promoting these other human nature arguments may use slightly differing terms for a similar aspect of the spirit/soul in their arguments from mind (consciousness, cognition, intelligence, rationality, feelings), will (desire, intentionality, aspirations, providential opportunities), beauty recognition, religious experience, love, and human greatness/misery (which relies on several aspects). Moreland argues the Theistic God's existence from human rational mind existence, asserting humanity's dualism (both physical body and non-physical soul, mind, or self exist), uniqueness of mental properties, and physicalism's failure to reasonably account for mind's origin from nothing or matter.[170] Deal and Holden identify an anthropological argument from intelligent beings to Intelligent Cause.[171] Walls and Dougherty edit a volume providing analysis of each of Plantinga's "two dozen (or so)" arguments for God plus a few more, including not only the four major categories but also at least four from mind (intentionality, cognition, intuition, consciousness), one from will/desire, and one from love.[172] Swinburne describes arguments from consciousness (private mental events including thought/feelings), providence (human responsibility to act on providential opportunities), and religious experience.[173] DeWeese and Moreland discuss the argument from religious experience (referencing Alston), and acknowledge arguments from human consciousness by Moreland and

---

170. J. P. Moreland, "God and the Argument from Mind," *Christian Apologetics: An Anthology of Primary Sources*, Eds. Khaldoun A. Sweis and Chad V. Meister (Grand Rapids, MI: Zondervan, 2012), 394-411.

171. Deal and Holden, "What Is the Overall Apologetic Task?," 45.

172. Walls and Dougherty, "Introduction," v-vii, 3-5.

173. Swinburne, *The Existence of God*, 192-212, 219, 293.

from human aspirations by Ganssle.[174] Alston argues the validity of religious experience, indicating belief formation from religious perception is similar to that from sensory perception while acknowledging that resulting beliefs must be judged for rationality.[175] Some, including Groothuis, describe a beauty (or aesthetic) argument, whereby objective beauty exists and theism best explains it; this might also be considered a design argument.[176] Groothuis also describes arguments from religious experience and human uniqueness (greatness, misery, consciousness, rationality).[177]

Natural Theology's Use during History

Natural theology has been used throughout Church history, with the term "natural theology" applied as early as Augustine (4th-5th century) for reasoning theism from general revelation.[178] When reasoning a natural theology argument, some authors mention the argument's historical connections; others do not. Historical overviews solely on natural theology are provided by some authors, such as Haines (*Natural Theology* work devoted to history, covering Classical to Reformation periods)[179] and Re Manning (edited volume with chapters on Classical to Modern periods).[180] Historical overviews for all apologetics are provided by other

---

174. DeWeese and Moreland, *Philosophy Made Slightly Less Difficult*, 189-192.

175. William Alston, "On Perceiving God," *Christian Apologetics: An Anthology of Primary Sources*, Eds. Khaldoun A. Sweis and Chad V. Meister (Grand Rapids, MI: Zondervan, 2012), 196-202.

176. Douglas Groothuis, *Christian Apologetics: A Comprehensive Case for Biblical Faith, 2nd Ed.* (Downers Grove, IL: InterVarsity Press, 2022), 257.

177. Groothuis, *Christian Apologetics* (2011), 21.

178. David Haines, *Natural Theology: A Biblical and Historical Introduction and Defense* (Landrum, SC: The Davenant Press, 2021), 12.

179. Ibid., 49-169.

180. Re Manning, Ed., *The Oxford Handbook of Natural Theology*, vii, 1.

authors, such as Boa and Bowman (chapter on Apostolic to Modern periods)[181] and Montgomery (opponent of natural theology with article covering Apostolic to Modern periods).[182] (Some authors such as Harrison, who defends McGrath's non-classical definition of natural theology, assert that the classical concept of it was "belatedly projected onto" the Christian tradition;[183] herein is no further discussion of that uncommon view.) This section is organized chronologically and does not consider biblical material.

Classical Greek and Roman Philosophy (500sBC-400sAD)

Some classical Greek and Roman philosophers, though having some faulty conclusions and not being pure theists (excepting probably Aristotle), argue natural theology elements, some of which are referenced later by Church natural theology proponents. Haines discusses such elements within four periods as follows. Greek Pre-Socratic philosophers (500sBC-400sBC) from universe contemplation concluded key attributes of God, including that there must be a single, original, fundamental first principle or cause and sustainer of everything that exists, with some calling this principle the "logos;" although, they might not have advocated more than pantheism's God-universe oneness.[184] The primary Greek Socratic philosophers (of the 400BCs-300BCs, influenced by Socrates) are Plato and Aristotle, with Plato describing God as "the intelligent, wise, powerful, and personal first principle or cause of the totality of the sensible universe and ground of morality" and Aristotle expressing a "classical monotheism" with God as the first unmoved mover who is "eternal, pure actuality, immutable, necessarily existing, alive,

---

181. Boa and Bowman, *Faith Has Its Reasons*, 9-32.

182. John Warwick Montgomery, "A Short History of Apologetics," *Christian Apologetics: An Anthology of Primary Sources*, Eds. Khaldoun A. Sweis and Chad V. Meister (Grand Rapids, MI: Zondervan, 2012), 21-28.

183. Harrison, "What is Natural Theology? (And Should We Dispense With It?)," 114.

184. Haines, *Natural Theology*, 49-56.

joyful and eternally happy, thought thinking itself, most good, immaterial, transcendent ..., unextended (i.e., omnipresent), absolutely simple ..., absolutely infinite, and impassible."[185] The Roman Post-Socratic philosopher Cicero (0sBC), a Stoic, articulated the innate human belief in existence of the divine, with the most potent reason (sometimes called the Ciceronian argument from Beauty) being that the beauty and order of the cosmos infer a Mind as artisan.[186] Roman pagan Neo-Platonists (0s-400sAD) further extended Platonic concepts, with Plotinus speaking of the One-Good being simple, immutable, eternal, and good and Proclus arguing both the One-Good as first cause from impossibility of infinite causal regress and man's purpose as entering union with the One-Good and needing divine assistance to do so.[187]

Apostolic Age (30AD-300AD)

The apologetics of early church fathers includes natural theology, sometimes using arguments promoted by Greek/Roman philosophers. Haines highlights Aristides (100sAD), whose *Apology* (possibly first post-N.T. apologetic work) refutes polytheism using arguments from Aristotle and Cicero, and Justin Martyr (100sAD) and Tertullian (100s-200sAD), who both argue that philosophy considering nature can bring men to "some" knowledge of the true God.[188] Boa and Bowman assert that "apologists of the second century modeled their arguments after contemporary philosophical refutations of polytheism and the critiques of pagan philosophy by Hellenistic Jews," noting that Justin was a convert from Platonism.[189] In Thorsteinsson's analysis

---

185. Ibid., 57-68.

186. Ibid., 68-73.

187. Ibid., 73-80.

188. Ibid., 81-87.

189. Boa and Bowman, *Faith Has Its Reasons*, 14.

of Justin's writings and conversion, he contends "Justin did not 'abandon philosophy' when he became a Christian," but rather held Christianity as the "only sure and useful philosophy."[190]

Early Middle Ages (300AD-1000AD)

In the Early Middle Ages church leaders include natural theology in theistic arguments. Haines' period history discusses the two Gregorys, Athanasius, and Augustine. Gregory Nazianzus and Gregory of Nyssa in the 300s indicate that considering nature can lead men to "some" knowledge of God, each adding various arguments such as from beauty/order.[191] Athanasius (300sAD) uses many arguments, including universe order with mutually dependent parts requiring a single Maker, the intelligent human soul requiring a Maker, and Cicero's beauty argument.[192] Augustine (300s-400sAD) provides arguments in various works indicating all men can and some do attain true knowledge that God exists and something of his nature; this knowledge is from natural, sensible observation and reasoning; and it is a preamble to belief in the Christian God.[193]

Augustine, as some earlier church leaders, was quite familiar with philosophy. He was converted after trying Manicheistic and Platonic philosophies, the latter of which helped point him to Christianity and is seen within his writings, including in cosmological arguments from

---

190. Runar Mar Thorsteinsson, "By Philosophy Alone: Reassessing Justin's Christianity and His Turn from Platonism," *Early Christianity* 3, no. 4 (2012), https://search-ebscohost-com.ezproxy.regent.edu/login.aspx?direct=true&db=rfh&AN=ATLA0001932400&site=ehost-live, 494, 516.

191. Haines, *Natural Theology*, 90-99.

192. Ibid., 87-90.

193. Ibid., 132.

creation to Creator God, according to Boa and Bowman.[194] Montgomery adds that Augustine "offered an apologetic of a Platonic nature to the intellectuals of his time."[195]

Late Middle and Renaissance Ages (1000AD-1500AD)

The church leaders of the Late Middle and Renaissance Ages most known for natural theology use are Anselm (1000s-1100s) and Thomas Aquinas (1200s). Anselm argues the "classic" ontological argument (though it contains a fallacy), according to Montgomery.[196] Boa and Bowman[197] (and others) observe the same.

Thomas Aquinas' natural theology arguments are "well-known," says Haines.[198] Montgomery notes that Aquinas argued from traditional proofs for God's existence from Aristotle.[199] Boa and Bowman concur, saying Aquinas created Christian philosophy from Aristotelian logic to fight his days' Greco-Arabic worldview challenges and is best known for arguing Theism from his "five ways."[200] He describes five natural theology arguments, four cosmological and one design. Cosmological arguments similar to Aquinas' are commonly termed "Thomistic."

Reformation and Enlightenment Ages (1500AD-1800AD)

In the basic philosophy of the original Reformers (1500s), "natural reason ... is still useful for about everything except what concerns salvation. Furthermore, they all are able to find

---

194. Boa and Bowman, *Faith Has Its Reasons*, 15-16.

195. Montgomery, "A Short History of Apologetics," 22.

196. Ibid., 23.

197. Boa and Bowman, *Faith Has Its Reasons*, 17.

198. Haines, *Natural Theology*, 142.

199. Montgomery, "A Short History of Apologetics," 23.

200. Boa and Bowman, *Faith Has Its Reasons*, 19-20.

a place for both natural theology and natural law," according to Haines.[201] Montgomery opines that the Reformers "were not concerned with apologetics as such" but rather with correct theology.[202] This seems plausible to some degree due to the Reformers' focus on reforming church doctrine and to the significant percentages of persons already believing in the Theistic God at that time. Haines expresses agreement with Turretin's opinion from the 1600s that at that time "in order to be orthodox one must teach 'there is a natural theology'" and provides evidence of natural theology in early Reformed theologians Calvin, Beza, Vermigli, Zanchi, Junius, Davenant, Turretin, and others, some noting differentiation between knowledge of God as Creator vs. as Redeemer.[203]

The Reformation was "firmly … steeped in classical theism," with Luther's (1500s) anti-Aristotelianism a minority position, according to Svensson.[204] Boa and Bowman assert that, while Luther agrees that reason can be useful for knowing God's existence, he holds that reason as emphasized by medieval theologians to argue Christianity was corrupting the gospel message.[205] Francisco's review of Luther's apologetics concludes that to Luther natural knowledge of God serves to keep "man from becoming brutes" by its reminder of an unattainable standard and by its encouragement to man to search for truth and God.[206]

---

201. David Haines, "The Use of Aquinas in Early Protestant Theology," *Without Excuse: Scripture, Reason, and Presuppositional Apologetics*, Ed. David Haines (Leesburg, VA: The Davenant Press, 2020), 228.

202. Montgomery, "A Short History of Apologetics," 23.

203. Haines, *Natural Theology*, 143, 145.

204. Manfred Svensson, "The Use of Aristotle in Early Protestant Theology," *Without Excuse: Scripture, Reason, and Presuppositional Apologetics*, Ed. David Haines (Leesburg, VA: The Davenant Press, 2020), 189, 197.

205. Boa and Bowman, *Faith Has Its Reasons*, 20-21.

206. Adam S. Francisco, "Luther's Use of Apologetics," *Concordia Theological Quarterly* 81, no. 3–4 (July 2017), https://search-ebscohost-com.ezproxy.regent.edu/login.aspx?direct=true&db=rfh&AN=ATLAiC9Y180604000035&site=ehost-live, 260.

Calvin (1500s) uses short, simple cosmological and teleological proofs for God's existence/attributes, according to Boa and Bowman, and argues that because of our innate sense of divinity (his *divinitatis sensum*) the doctrine of God's existence is mastered by all from birth and is not able to be forgotten due to nature though many so strive.[207] Possibly Calvin's minimal natural theology use contributes to some modern theologians believing Calvin did not allow any natural theology.[208]

Between Aquinas of the Middle Ages and Locke (1600s-1700s) of the Enlightenment, "a vast change of mentality occurred" philosophically in the Church, from natural theology to an evidentialist apologetics focus, according to Wolterstorff.[209] Influences toward such a change, however much it is true, may have included the Reformation focus on Church doctrine rather than evangelism and the Enlightenment focus on accurate reasoning for everything. Strong evidential arguments may have become more beneficial late in the Enlightenment after, according to Boa and Bowman, anti-Christian Hume (1700s) had convinced many that all Christian apologetic arguments, including all natural theology, were unsound.[210] Sennett and Groothuis assert that Hume's empiricism still influences philosophy, saying, "the supposed Humean refutation of the [natural theology] enterprise is a myth whose exposure is long overdue."[211]

---

207. Boa and Bowman, *Faith Has Its Reasons*, 224.

208. Ibid.

209. Nicholas Wolterstorff, "The Migration of the Theistic Arguments: From Natural Theology to Evidentialist Apologetics," In *Rationality, Religious Belief, and Moral Commitment: New Essays in the Philosophy of Religion*, Ithaca, NY, 1986, https://search-ebscohost-com.ezproxy.regent.edu/login.aspx?direct=true&db=rfh&AN=ATLA0001146970&site=ehost-live, 38, 79.

210. Boa and Bowman, *Faith Has Its Reasons*, 23.

211. James F. Sennett and Douglas Groothuis, "Introduction," *In Defense of Natural Theology: A Post-Humean Assessment*, Eds. James F. Sennett and Douglas Groothuis (Downers Grove, IL: InterVarsity Press, 2005), 9, 15.

Modern Age (1800AD-2000AD)

Natural theology has been used within Modern Age apologetics. Paley's *Natural Theology* of the early 1800s was in Craig's view "the high point in the development of the teleological argument prior to our time."[212] Boa and Bowman note that later in the century Paley's argument was weakened for many by Darwin's naturalistic arguments.[213]

Concerning debate of recent centuries on natural theology views amongst Reformed theologians, Haines concludes that most early reformers believed it valid while various but not all later Reformed theologians believed it invalid.[214] For example, Hodge (1800s), a famous Calvinist theologian at Princeton, thinks traditional natural theology arguments valid.[215] Sudduth, in his volume focused on refuting the three main arguments of the so-called Reformed theological objection to natural theology, says "contrary to a widely held opinion in contemporary philosophy of religion, the Reformed theological tradition exhibits a deeply entrenched and historically continuous endorsement of natural theology."[216]

Various major natural theology proponents of the Modern Age are critiqued both by Boa and Bowman[217] and by several authors in Re Manning's volume.[218] As in other ages, the age's culture impacted how natural theology arguments were received and crafted. For example, Eddy points out that the pervasive evil and moral devastation of World War I caused existential

---

212. Craig, *Reasonable Faith*, 101.

213. Boa and Bowman, *Faith Has Its Reasons*, 24.

214. Haines, *Natural Theology*, 9.

215. Boa and Bowman, *Faith Has Its Reasons*, 24.

216. Michael Sudduth, *The Reformed Objection to Natural Theology* (New York, NY: Routledge, 2016), 6, 9.

217. Boa and Bowman, *Faith Has Its Reasons*, 23-32.

218. Re Manning, Ed., *The Oxford Handbook of Natural Theology*, 75-134.

bewilderment and weakened the appeal of natural theology arguments;[219] the same might be said of World War II and other cases of extreme evil. Recent natural theology work is discussed elsewhere (as in previous approaches and arguments sections).

Nontheistic Worldviews Today

Apologists may classify today's prominent nontheistic worldviews differently and suggest differing considerations for engaging with their beliefs. Some authors do not describe any nontheistic worldviews, but simply describe the Christian worldview as they think it best communicated (e.g., Rasmussen,[220] who uses many natural theology arguments). Many classical apologists do not provide recommendations on applying specific natural theology arguments for specific worldview classifications; although some do. All natural theology arguments might be useful in light of any worldview because no nontheistic worldview acknowledges the personal Creator God.

While various worldview classifications exist, this section considers the following classifications (except theism) because of their prominence in apologist literature:

Modernism – which commonly views objective truth as knowable only by human reason, with no God; sometimes classified by the **Naturalism/Matterism** (all is matter) derived from it

Postmodernism – which commonly views current truth as socially constructed using human language and objective truth as unknowable or non-existent, with no God

Monism – which commonly views truth as existing within the oneness of everything, which is God, and as revealed in certain circumstances; sometimes classified as **Pantheism/Mindism**; variants include **New Age** (every human is God) and **Buddhism and some Hindu sects** (every human is nothing)

---

219. Matthew D. Eddy, "Nineteenth-century Natural Theology," *The Oxford Handbook of Natural Theology*, Ed. Russell Re Manning (Oxford, U.K.: Oxford University Press, 2013), 114.

220. Rasmussen, *How Reason Can Lead to God*.

Theism – which views objective truth as revealed by the personal Creator God using general and special revelation which include reason and faith

Agnosticism and apatheism are not considered separately because many of their adherents generally also adhere at least weakly to one of the above classifications. Geisler identifies agnosticism as claiming either that the existence and nature of God are not known or are unknowable.[221] He observes agnostic elements within modernist and postmodernist materials.[222] Beshears identifies apatheism (apathy toward God) as "indifference and apathy toward the existence of God," from feeling "a sense of existential security absent God."[223] He suggests initial communication with apatheists may not be helped by ontological, teleological, and transcendental arguments; rather, we should, as Schaeffer's pre-evangelism promotes, first help them doubt their beliefs by uncovering points of tension in their logical end, including in areas of love, beauty, meaning, significance, and truth.[224] Those areas coincide with concepts of some anthropological natural theology arguments.

Because individuals' worldviews are unique and few "have well-articulated worldviews,"[225] our communication should be unique to the individuals or audience. Groothuis correctly observes that "while the technical discussions of worldviews fall into set categories … people's beliefs are not always that well categorized. … people hold a smorgasbord of beliefs …

---

221. Geisler, *Christian Apologetics, 2nd Ed.*, 3.

222. Ibid., 3-10.

223. Kyle Beshears, "Athens without a Statue to the Unknown God," *Themelios* 44, no. 3 (December 2019): 517–29, https://search-ebscohost-com.ezproxy.regent.edu/login.aspx?direct=true&db=rfh&AN=ATLAiACO191216000974&site=ehost-live, 517.

224. Ibid., 526, 528.

225. Groothuis, *Christian Apologetics* (2011), 77.

There may be a dash of Christianity ... heaps of New Age spirituality ... a dose of naturalism ... and ... substantial seasoning by relativism."[226]

Modernism (Naturalism/Matterism) and Postmodernism

Most classical apologist authors identify modernism and postmodernism as the two predominant nontheistic worldview classifications of recent centuries, particularly in Western culture. These classifications are considered herein together because they are frequently described together and compared. Modernism (Enlightenment worldview) dominated for centuries, then postmodernism advanced to prominence, with Kelly and Dew identifying "the year 1968 as the pivotal turning point in the final transition from modern to postmodern."[227] Authors discussing these classifications and related apologetic approaches include Kelly and Dew, Sennett and Groothuis, Moreland and Craig, Groothuis, Chan, DeWeese and Moreland, Gould, Boa and Bowman, Chatraw, and Koukl.

Kelly and Dew provide an entire work analyzing postmodernism, including significant comparison with modernism.[228] They characterize modernism as committed to five core beliefs, of which the key may be the "high level of confidence in human reason and in the human ability to know reality with certainty"[229] by discovering reality. They characterize postmodernism as committed to ten core beliefs, of which the keys may be its challenge to confidence in human reason and view of "truth as something that is created/constructed by human beings, rather than something discovered."[230] Concerning how humans come to beliefs relative to reason, radical

---

226. Ibid., 42-43.

227. Kelly and Dew, *Understanding Postmodernism*, 2.

228. Ibid.

229. Ibid., 29.

230. Ibid., 4-5, 9.

modernists say humans can be purely rational and set aside social/emotional factors, radical postmodernists say humans are purely nonrational and social/emotional factors cause belief, and theists understand humans as modestly rational with both reason and social/emotional factors considered.[231] Postmodernists commonly believe "there may be a true story (worldview), but we humans are unable to know it," thus causing objections to Christianity's substantial truth claims.[232] Christians can refute both modernism's complete dependence on human rationality and postmodernism's complete lack of trust in human rationality, both of which reject the possibility of an alternative source of truth beyond humanity.

Because ideas of Hume, an eighteenth-century empiricist (stemming from modernism) philosopher, exist in "virtually all topical introductions to philosophy" and still strongly influence nontheistic philosophy, Sennett and Groothuis provide an edited work analyzing Hume's empiricism.[233] The work defends against Hume's attacks on natural theology. For example, Penelhum asserts that Hume's empiricism fails to permit the idea of a unique final (i.e., first) cause.[234]

Moreland and Craig indicate that their entire *Philosophical Foundations* work is essentially "a critique of and an alternative to postmodernism."[235] They consider postmodernism "a form of cultural relativism about such things as reality, truth, reason, value, linguistic meaning, the self, and other notions," explaining it in seven aspects (including reality being a

---

231. Ibid., 44-45, 62-63.

232. Ibid., 188, 223.

233. Sennett and Groothuis, "Introduction," *In Defense of Natural Theology*, 9-10.

234. Terence Penelhum, "Hume's Criticisms of Natural Theology," *In Defense of Natural Theology: A Post-Humean Assessment*, Eds. James F. Sennett and Douglas Groothuis (Downers Grove, IL: InterVarsity Press, 2005), 40-41.

235. Moreland and Craig, *Philosophical Foundations for a Christian Worldview, 2nd Ed.*, 136.

social construction created by language) while acknowledging that it is a "loose coalition of diverse thinkers."[236] While postmodernists correctly warn of dangers of abused modernism in excesses of scientism and authoritarianism, theists can refute postmodernism's main tenets due to its untrue claim that everyone's rational objectivity is biased and to it being self-refuting (saying its own assertions are true/rational and rejecting obvious truths existing separate from language including mathematical).[237] Moreland and Craig promote cosmological, teleological, axiological (moral), and ontological natural theology arguments as potential parts of theistic response.[238]

Groothuis asserts that both modernism and postmodernism have contributed, each in their own way, to "truth decay," which he defines as the "cultural condition in which the very idea of absolute, objective and universal truth is considered implausible, [contemptable], or [ignored]."[239] Modernism's presuppositions about human reason discovering all objective truth require rejecting religion and spiritual reality,[240] so Christians can agree with modernists on truth's existence and discoverability but refute their stance on truth's source and existence of spiritual truth. Postmodernism's presuppositions about social construction of truth require rejecting its connection with objective reality,[241] so Christians can agree with postmodernists that modernism does not answer some primary questions but refute postmodernists' stance on objective truth not existing by pointing out that not only do certain objective truths exist (e.g.,

---

236. Ibid., 132-133.

237. Ibid., 136-139.

238. Ibid., 475-509.

239. Groothuis, *Truth Decay*, 22, 32.

240. Ibid., 35, 38.

241. Groothuis, *Christian Apologetics* (2011), 128.

mathematical) but also postmodernists live in many life aspects as if they do. Interestingly, Groothuis indicates that not only do modernists claim to be naturalists (only the physical exists), which matches their philosophy, but also many postmodernists claim the same, though for them this must be a preference or prejudice rather than their philosophical position.[242] Groothuis promotes at least the cosmological, teleological, and moral natural theology arguments as potential parts of the Christian response to postmodernists in his *Truth Decay* work,[243] and a full range of natural theology arguments in his *Christian Apologetics* work.[244]

Chan describes modernism (all truth) and postmodernism (all interpretation, a "reaction" to modernism") by analyzing six primary features of each.[245] For best addressing modernists, he employs the sequence Christianity is true, so you must believe, so you must live it; whereas for postmodernists, his sequence is Christianity is livable, so it is believable, so it is true.[246] Chan states that although the NT communication approach to Jews focuses on common ground of scripture, the approach to Gentiles focuses on common ground of God's common graces, general revelation, universal human desires, and their cultural authors.[247] Chan does not describe specific natural theology arguments, but they would be part of his general revelation and universal human desires categories.

---

242. Groothuis, *Truth Decay*, 38.

243. Ibid., 180.

244. Groothuis, *Christian Apologetics* (2011).

245. Sam Chan, *Evangelism in a Skeptical World: How to Make the Unbelievable News About Jesus More Believable* (Grand Rapids, MI: Zondervan, 2018), 101-115.

246. Ibid., 125.

247. Ibid., 67.

Classical apologists who acknowledge postmodernism/modernism but discuss them less extensively include DeWeese and Moreland, Gould, Boa and Bowman, Chatraw, and Koukl. DeWeese and Moreland classify Christianity's two major Western worldview opponents as postmodernism, which rejects objective truth or ability to know it, and scientific naturalism, which rejects the immaterial soul.[248] (Naturalism stems from modernism's rationality.) DeWeese and Moreland's "philosophy of religion" includes these natural theology arguments: ontological, cosmological, design, moral, religious experience, human consciousness, and human aspirations.[249] Gould likewise classifies Christianity's two Western worldview opponents as postmodernism (victimhood due to socially constructed reality and oppression of powerful) and naturalism (meaninglessness due to material world and vulnerable selves).[250] His apologetic approach of a narrative from three universal longings of the human soul (truth to reason, goodness to conscience, and beauty to imagination) employs natural theology arguments including human desire, beauty, reason, moral, and cosmological.[251] Boa and Bowman (who may not be classical apologists, but describe it and other approaches) summarize postmodernism as a "cultural movement that has applied relativistic thinking" (all truth is relative to the perspective) "in various fields of thought ... even theology," adding that classical apologists "resist relativism in all its forms as a logically incoherent view of knowledge."[252] Chatraw discusses characteristics of modernism (especially reason and scientific method) and postmodernism (especially

---

248. DeWeese and Moreland, *Philosophy Made Slightly Less Difficult*, 198.

249. Ibid., 177-192.

250. Paul M. Gould, *Cultural Apologetics: Renewing the Christian Voice, Conscience, and Imagination in a Disenchanted World* (Grand Rapids, MI: Zondervan, 2019), 206-208.

251. Ibid., 29, 75, 104, 130, 156, 185.

252. Boa and Bowman, *Faith Has Its Reasons*, 74.

individualism and skepticism leading to meaninglessness, sometimes calling it late modernism), indicating that they are not total opposites because for both "the individual 'self' still rules" and both (like Christianity) are meta-stories "accepted in part by faith of some kind."[253] Because "God made us to connect with and through stories," his apologetic approach emphasizes a narrative imagining a better human meaning, self, happiness, inclusiveness, and reason, and weaves in natural theology arguments including design/cosmological, beauty, moral, mind, and others.[254] Koukl uses the term matterism to describe what many others term naturalism or materialism, while saying that it and mindism are the two major competing stories to Christianity, which believes matter and mind are real.[255] He interweaves various natural theology arguments, including beauty and moral, within his story approach to apologetics.[256]

Monism (Pantheism/Mindism)

Some classical apologist authors identify monism (sometimes termed pantheism or mindism) as a nontheistic worldview classification that, although originating primarily in Eastern culture, is increasingly common in Western culture as Eastern/Western cultures intermix. While all of its variants view all things (including truth) as existing within the oneness (or one mind) of everything, which is God, it has main variants whereby in one every human is nothing (including Buddhism and some Hindu sects) and in the other every human is God (including New Age). Classical apologist authors who discuss this classification include Koukl, Schaeffer, and Groothuis.

---

253. Joshua D. Chatraw, *Telling a* Better *Story: How to Talk About God in a Skeptical Age* (Grand Rapids, MI: Zondervan, 2020), 27-33.

254. Ibid., ix, 41, 44-45, 49.

255. Koukl, *The Story of Reality*, 53, 56.

256. Ibid., 75-86.

Koukl uses the term mindism to describe what many others term monism or pantheism, identifying it and matterism as the two major competing stories to Christianity.[257] He highlights that while mindism appears very open-minded by allowing many routes to enlightenment, in the end it is narrow, with its God as real and all else an imagination, with you being nothing in one variant and your suffering being your own fault in the other.[258] As noted previously, Koukl interweaves various natural theology arguments, including beauty and moral, within his story-based communication approach.[259]

Schaeffer specifies pantheism, which he also called pan-everythingism, as a significant worldview of which to be aware when he identifies (last century) in pop music (e.g., the Beatles) a "vague pantheism which predominates much of the new mystical thought."[260] "Beginning with the impersonal, everything, including man, must be explained in terms of the impersonal plus time plus chance;" and according to Schaeffer this explanation applies to pantheism's modern scientific form (naturalism) "which reduces everything to energy particles."[261] He emphasizes that before acknowledging sin and faith one must acknowledge there is an infinite-personal Creator and I am His creature, therefore "pre-evangelism" may be required for that to occur.[262] While Schaeffer seems an evidentialist, his pre-evangelism approach integrates concepts from natural theology arguments (e.g., cosmological, design, moral).

---

257. Ibid., 56.

258. Ibid., 57-60.

259. Ibid., 75-86.

260. Schaeffer, *The Francis A. Schaeffer Trilogy*, 41, 60.

261. Ibid., 283.

262. Ibid., 146, 154.

Groothuis asserts that pantheism's one mind philosophy is deficient in various ways, including that it "cannot explain key features of the universe and human persons" and it renders love an illusion because the loveless impersonal is ultimate reality.[263] Natural theology arguments can provide alternatives to various deficiencies. As noted previously, Groothuis promotes a full range of natural theology arguments.[264]

---

263. Groothuis, *Christian Apologetics* (2011), 53, 84.

264. Ibid.

CHAPTER 3: NATURAL THEOLOGY IN SCRIPTURE

This chapter examines key Scripture passages related to natural theology, including exegesis of Romans 1:18-20, discussion of Acts on Paul's gentile apologetic encounters, and discussion of various other OT and NT passages. God speaks through both nature and Scripture, with "the written book of God constantly [bearing] witness to God's other book, the book of nature," as Haines and Fulford assert. Scripture indicates not only things God expects people to observe through general revelation but also what God expects people to reason from those observations, including acknowledging Him as God and every person accountable to Him. For, as Groothuis says, "The ruler of the universe ... deigns to reason with his creatures who are made in his image and who, therefore, share (in a finite and fallible way) the ability to reason."[265]

Scripture passages have differing relationships to natural theology argumentation. Nitzsch correlates the major natural theology arguments to some key scriptures in this way: cosmological – Romans 1:20; teleological – Psalm 8, Acts 14:17; moral – Romans 2:14; and ontological – Acts 17:24, Romans 1:19, 32.[266] Others may correlate differently. Some passages, such as Romans 1, use natural theology in support of doctrine. Others, such as Acts 14/17, use it within dialogue of believers with unbelievers. Still others, such as Job, use it within dialogue amongst God-fearers and within monologue of God to men. While natural theology arguments are from general revelation, when such arguments are referenced in Scripture, whether directly stated or indirectly assumed, this author considers those references as containing both general and special revelation, with special revelation confirming the general.

---

265. Groothuis, *Christian Apologetics* (2011), 31.

266. Sudduth, *The Reformed Objection to Natural Theology*, on Bavinck noting Nitzsch, 161.

Natural theology objectors argue using their interpretation of certain Scripture passages, with some noted previously. Some use Colossians 2:8 to condemn all philosophical reasoning, but Paul specifically condemns only that which is not "in accordance with Christ." Other objectors interpret various passages from a perspective of sin's strong noetic effects to condemn natural theology. According to Groothuis, however, "the orthodox natural theologian claims that the relevance of noetic impairment concerns a tendency to attempt to escape God's authority in various ways but that this does not entail the failure of natural theology."[267]

Natural Theology's Gospel Relevance in Romans 1:18-20: An Exegesis

Romans 1:18-20, by highlighting the critical relationship between God's wrath and human suppression of God's general revelation, suggests potential relevance of natural theology for gospel communication; thus, an exegesis is provided. 1:18-20 (NASB2020) says:

> 18 For the wrath of God is revealed from heaven
>   against all ungodliness and unrighteousness of people
>   who suppress the truth in unrighteousness,
> 19 because that which is known about God
>   is evident within them; for God made it evident to them.
> 20 For since the creation of the world His invisible *attributes,*
>   *that is,* His eternal power and divine nature,
>   have been clearly perceived, being understood by what has been made,
>   so that they are without excuse.

The pericope summarizes both truth of God's general revelation to all people through His creation and that truth's sufficiency to require accountability to live righteously before Him as our personal God. "The *locus classico* for natural theology, without question, is Romans 1," according to Haines and Fulford.[268] This exegesis' organization includes the pericope's place

---

267. Douglas R. Groothuis, "Proofs, Pride, and Incarnation: Is Natural Theology Theologically Taboo?," *Journal of the Evangelical Theological Society* 38, no. 1 (March 1995): 67–76, https://search-ebscohost-com.ezproxy.regent.edu/login.aspx?direct=true&db=rfh&AN=ATLA0000899152&site=ehost-live, 69-70.

268. Haines and Fulford, *Natural Law*, 87.

within the broader context of Romans (especially chapters 1 to 4), the structure and main motifs of this and surrounding pericopes, a detailed exegesis, and the main message summary with some objections noted.

Place of Romans 1:18-20 Within Broader Context of Romans

Paul's letter to the Romans can be outlined as follows for purposes of this exegesis. This outline is that of this author.

An Outline of Romans:

- **1:1-15**   PROLOGUE – PAUL'S EAGERNESS TO SHARE THE GOSPEL:
  Paul is motivated in the gospel by his call, service, and obligation.
- **1:16-17**   THE GOSPEL'S UNIVERSAL OFFER SUMMARY:
  God's gospel is available to all for salvation in righteousness by faith.
- **1:18-3:20**   THE UNIVERSAL HUMAN PROBLEM WITH GOD:
  God's wrath and judgment of eternal death (separation) is against all because of ungodliness/unrighteousness due to sin against God.
  - **1:18-20**   **God's Wrath is Revealed Against Ungodliness/Unrighteousness for Suppressing Truth of God's General Revelation Evident Within.**
  - **1:21-23**   Ungodliness/unrighteousness of those suppressing God's truth includes not honoring/thanking Him and futility/darkness/foolishness/idolatry.
  - **1:24-32**   God judges those living ungodly/unrighteous by giving them up to impurity, degradation, and depravity of mind and deed.
  - **2:1-3:20**   God impartially judges everyone's unrighteous behavior, whether having God's moral law (as Jews) or not, for works of law make none righteous and increase responsibility due to knowing sin.
- **3:21-4:25**   THE GOSPEL AS ONLY SOLUTION TO HUMAN PROBLEM WITH GOD:
  God gives righteousness only through faith in Christ's work.
  - **3:21-31**   Righteousness (justification) through faith in Christ's propitiatory death is only provided to all who believe apart from works of moral law.
  - **4:1-25**   Righteousness through faith is exemplified in OT by Abraham.
- **5:1-8:39**   THE GOSPEL'S NEW LIFE PROVIDED BY GOD'S RIGHTEOUSNESS:
  Righteousness through faith provides new life within to reign in life.
  - **5:1-5:11**   Righteousness through faith means living in peace/joy/hope/love.
  - **5:12-7:25**   Righteousness through faith means living dead to (freed from) sin's and law's bondages and alive to God due to grace's power.
  - **8:1-8:39**   Righteousness through faith means living as conquerors (even of suffering) due to Spirit indwelling and God's love.
- **9:1-11:36**   THE GOSPEL FOR ISRAEL:
  Jews remain part of God's plan and must respond by faith for salvation.
- **12:1-15:13**   THE GOSPEL LIVED:
  Believers are called to living as a sacrifice in service to God.
- **15:14-16:27**   EPILOGUE - THE GOSPEL IN ACTION:

Paul provides final personal encouragements, plans, and greetings.

This Romans outline specifies eight first level pericopes, each using the word "gospel," a keyword within the book. It is common opinion that Paul's gospel summary statement in 1:16-17 is the theme of the book, according to Moo.[269] In summary, God's gospel provides salvation to all who believe through righteousness by faith in Christ's works.

In three first level pericopes of Romans, Paul specifies the gospel's critical aspects, which are its universal offer summary (1:16-17), the universal human unrighteousness problem with God that requires it (1:18-3:20), and the only solution being its core tenet that faith in Christ's work alone provides righteousness (3:21-4:25). The starts of each indicate something of God being "revealed," righteousness in the first and third and wrath in the second. Three other first level pericopes explain the gospel's consequences to new life within, Israel, and living with others. The remaining two provide prologue and epilogue.

Multiple commentators identify 1:18-3:20 as a unified pericope explaining the human unrighteousness problem that requires the gospel's solution, starting with its 1:18-20 summary of the human unrighteousness problem followed by further detail of specific unrighteousness and God's judgment.[270,271,272] This author uses these sub-pericopes:

1:18-20   God's wrath is against ungodliness/unrighteousness for suppressing truth of general revelation
1:21-23   Those suppressing that truth live in ungodliness/unrighteousness
1:24-32   God's judges that sin by giving over to additional unrighteousness
2:1-3:20 God's impartially judges all men including those having His moral law

---

269. Douglas J. Moo, *The Letter to the Romans, 2nd Ed.*, The New International Commentary on the New Testament (Grand Rapids, Mich.: Eerdmans, 2018), 67.

270. Ibid., 102.

271. John R. W. Stott, *The Message of Romans: God's Good News for the World*, The Bible Speaks Today (Downers Grove, Ill.: InterVarsity Press, 1994), 67.

272. F. F. Bruce, *Romans: An Introduction and Commentary*, Tyndale New Testament Commentaries 6 (Downers Grove, Ill.: InterVarsity Press, 1985), 88.

Some commentators differ on sub-pericope breakdown.

Regarding breakdown of 1:21-32, which delineates specific unrighteousness, Boa and Kruidenier use a similar two-part breakdown as this author.[273] Moo differs in a non-critical way by splitting it into 1:21-31 on all unrighteous consequences and 1:32 as a conclusion.[274] Stott's breakdown into 1:21-24, 1:25-27, and 1:28-32 is also a non-critical difference.[275]

Regarding 2:1-3:20, this author believes it focuses on judgment and moral law for all having God's moral law (including Jews) and can be considered as one set, but some commentators differ, saying all or some applies to Jews only or to everyone. This suggests theological differences which are not significant relative to 1:18-20's exegesis unless one believes 1:18-32 applies to gentiles only, such as Johnson,[276] in which case one believes that 1:18-20's general revelation suppression is only relevant to unbelieving gentiles. Horne notes that Paul does not speak of Jews and gentiles except in 2:14-29; therefore, the prior and following verses of 1:18-3:20 apply to everyone, not just gentiles.[277] Boa and Kruidenier make 2:1-3:20 a separate first level pericope and title it specific to Jews, but allow for 1:18-32 to apply to everyone.[278] Moo makes sub-pericopes with 2:1-3:8 titled specific to Jews and the rest to

---

273. Kenneth Boa and William Kruidenier, *Romans*, Holman New Testament Commentary (Nashville: Broadman and Holman Publishers, 2000), 66.

274. Moo, *The Letter to the Romans*, 107.

275. Stott, *The Message of Romans*, 76-79.

276. S. Lewis Johnson, "Paul and the Knowledge of God," *Bibliotheca Sacra* 129, no. 513 (January 1972): 61–74, https://search-ebscohost-com.ezproxy.regent.edu/login.aspx?direct=true&db=rfh&AN=ATLA0000730528&site=ehost-live, 64.

277. Charles M. Horne, "Toward a Biblical Apologetic," *Bulletin of the Evangelical Theological Society* 4, no. 3 (November 1961): 89–92, https://search-ebscohost-com.ezproxy.regent.edu/login.aspx?direct=true&db=rfh&AN=ATLA0000669998&site=ehost-live, 89.

278. Boa and Kruidenier, *Romans*, 69.

everyone,[279] while Stott and Bruce both make sub-pericopes with 2:17-3:8 titled specific to Jews, 2:1-16 to moralizers, and the rest to everyone.[280,281]

Structure and Main Motifs of Romans 1:18-20 and Surrounding Pericopes

The structure and main motifs of Romans 1:18-20 and of its most closely surrounding pericopes shed light on its meaning. Analysis includes one first level preceding pericope, 1:16-17, due to its gospel summary providing insight on 1:18-20's human unrighteousness problem summary. It also includes the first three of 1:18-3:20's four sub-pericopes, covering 1:18-32, because the two following 1:18-20 explain details of the scope of unrighteousness identified in 1:18-20. The fourth sub-pericope, covering 2:1-3:20, could provide additional insight but is excluded due to space limitations herein.

The Romans 1:16-32 text follows, structured in its pericopes and sub-pericopes, with key terms indicating main motifs highlighted by bolding and underlining unique to the motif.

1:16-17 (pericope 2)
16 For I am not ashamed of the gospel, for it is the power of God for salvation
    to everyone who believes, to the Jew first and also to the Greek.
17 For in it *the* **righteousness** of God is revealed from faith to faith;
    as it is written: "BUT THE **RIGHTEOUS** *ONE* WILL LIVE BY FAITH."

1:18-20 (pericope 3, sub-pericope 1)
18 For the **wrath of God is revealed** from heaven
    against all **ungodliness** and **unrighteousness**
    of people who suppress the truth in **unrighteousness**,
19 because that which is known about God
    is evident within them; for God made it evident to them.
20 For since the creation of the world
    His invisible *attributes, that is,* His eternal power and divine nature,
    have been clearly perceived, being understood by what has been made,
    so that they are without excuse.

---

279. Moo, *The Letter to the Romans*, 135, 206.

280. Stott, *The Message of Romans*, 68.

281. Bruce, *Romans*, 73.

1:21-23 (pericope 3, sub-pericope 2)
21 For even though they knew God, they did not honor Him as God or give thanks,
> but they became futile in their reasonings, and their senseless hearts were darkened.
22 Claiming to be wise, they became fools,
23 and they exchanged the glory of the incorruptible God for an image in the form of
> corruptible mankind, of birds, four-footed animals, and crawling creatures.

1:24-32 (pericope 3, sub-pericope 3)
24 Therefore, **God gave them up** to vile impurity in the lusts of their hearts,
> so that their bodies would be dishonored among them.
25 For they exchanged the truth of God for falsehood, and worshiped and served
> the creature rather than the Creator, who is blessed forever. Amen.
26 For this reason **God gave them over** to degrading passions;
> for their women exchanged natural relations for that which is contrary to nature,
27 and likewise the men, too, abandoned natural relations with women and
>> burned in their desire toward one another, males with males committing shameful acts
>> and receiving in their own persons the due penalty of their error.
28 And just as they did not see fit to acknowledge God,
> **God gave them up** to a depraved mind, to do those things that are not proper,
29 *people* having been filled with all unrighteousness, wickedness, greed, *and* evil;
> full of envy, murder, strife, deceit, *and* malice; they are gossips,
30 slanderers, haters of God, insolent, arrogant, boastful, inventors of evil,
> disobedient to parents,
31 without understanding, untrustworthy, unfeeling, *and* unmerciful;
32 and although they know the ordinance of God,
>> that those who practice such things are worthy of death,
>> they not only do the same, but also approve of those who practice them.

The table following summarizes main motifs of Romans 1:18-20 and of surrounding text inclusive of 1:16-1:32. Specified are the motif title, the terms within the text indicative of the motif, the verses where each term is used, and the number of occurrences of each term both total and within each sub-pericope.

Romans 1:16-32 (NASB2020) Main Motifs With Related Terms/Verses	# Total	# in 1:16-17	# in 1:18-20	# in 1:21-23	# in 1:24-32
Motif A: wrath/judgment	4		1		3
-wrath of God revealed: 18	1		1		
-God gave them over/up: 24, 26, 28	3				3

Motif B1: righteousness	**2**	**2**			
-righteousness, righteous: 17, 17	2	2			
Motif B2: ungodliness/unrighteousness	**many**		**3**	**many**	**many**
-ungodliness: 18	1		1		
-unrighteousness: 18, 18	2		2		
-[examples of ungodli./unright. in 21-32]	many			many	many
Motif C1: truth known to all from nature	**8**		**4**	**1**	**3**
-truth (of God): 18, 25	2		1		1
-(truth known about) God: 19, 21, 28	3		1	1	1
-His invisible *attributes, that is*, His eternal power and divine nature: 20	1		1		
-what has been made: 20	1		1		
-ordinance of God, that those who practice such things are worthy of death: 32	1				1
Motif C2: having knowledge of truth known to all	**7**		**5**	**1**	**1**
-known: 19	1		1		
-evident, made evident: 19, 19	2		2		
-clearly perceived: 20	1		1		
-understood: 20	1		1		
-knew/know: 21, 32	2			1	1
Motif C3: suppressing knowledge of truth known to all	**7**		**1**	**2**	**4**
-suppress: 18	1		1		
-did not honor Him … or give thanks: 21	1			1	
-exchanged … for an image: 23	1			1	
-exchanged for falsehood: 25	1				1
-exchanged for that which is contrary to nature: 26	1				1
-abandoned [natural] and burned: 27	1				1
-did not acknowledge: 28	1				1
Motif C4: accountability for suppressing knowledge of truth known to all	**1**		**1**		
-without excuse: 20	1		1		

Romans 1:18-20 and its broader context of 1:16-32 contain these three sets of main motifs: (A) wrath/judgment [underlined bold text], (B) the two-item contrasting set of righteousness and ungodliness/unrighteousness [bold text], and (C) the four-item set related to

truth known to all humans by what has been made [text underlined in one of four ways]. 1:18-20 incorporates all of these sets of motifs. Motif set B connects 1:16-17 and 1:18-20 because the former emphasizes the righteousness of the gospel's solution and the latter the unrighteousness of the human problem. Motif set C connects 1:18-20 with 1:21-23 and 1:24-32 because of the commonality of set items. All three 1:18-32 sub-pericopes contain examples from three of motif set C items: truth known, having knowledge of truth, and suppressing knowledge of truth. The fourth motif set C item, accountability for suppressing knowledge of truth, occurs only clearly within 1:18-20.

Because the above motif table is intended to identify the most significant motifs and terms, changing it slightly to include or exclude certain items based on slightly differing interpretations would not change its usefulness. For example, motif set C1 might add "natural relations" (1:26-27) because this is "natural" (understood from nature), but some may wish to exclude it as not being primary known truth.

Romans 1:18-20 Detailed Exegesis

This section provides detailed exegesis of the Romans 1:18-20 text organized by its main motifs noted in the previous section, which are:

- (A)   Wrath/judgment
- (B2) Ungodliness/unrighteousness
- (C1) Truth known to all from nature
- (C2) Having knowledge of truth known to all
- (C3) Suppressing knowledge of truth known to all
- (C4) Accountability for suppressing knowledge of truth known to all

Its message as a whole is discussed in the next section.

God's wrath (motif A) means *what* in 1:18? Wrath (*orge*) is "strong indignation directed at wrongdoing, with focus on retribution," specifically here "God's indignation against sin in the present."[282] Moo spotlights God's character, stating, "wrath is an aspect of God's person ... He cannot behold with indifference that His creation is destroyed and His holy will trodden underfoot. Therefore he meets sin with His mighty and annihilating reaction."[283] Wrath "is not vindictive rage, nor is it an emotional reaction to irritated self-concern," reminds Johnson.[284] Boa and Kruidenier distinguish wrath and judgment, which are sometimes confused and are both within 1:18-3:20, as follows: "Wrath comes as a result of judgment (a decision), and judgment comes as a result of comparison with a standard. Therefore, God's wrath is always a function of his having judged something against the standard of his righteousness or his established order."[285] God expresses wrath both in the present (already) and in the future at the present age's end (not yet), but the present tense of 1:18's "is revealed" indicates this is at least present revelation. Moo explains, "although God will inflict his wrath on sin finally and irrevocably at the end of time (2:5) ... as vv. 24-28 suggest, the wrath of God is now visible in his 'handing over' of human beings to their chosen way of sin and all its consequences."[286] Commentators differ on how God causes the "handing over," ranging from direct action in the person to removal of grace and letting degradation occur.[287,288] Paul speaks of future wrath in 2:1-3:20 when addressing the morally arrogant, declaring such a person is "storing up wrath for yourself on the day of wrath and revelation of the righteous judgment of God" (2:5).

---

282. Walter Bauer, *A Greek-English Lexicon of the New Testament and Other Early Christian Literature*, Ed. Frederick W. Danker, 3rd Ed. (Chicago: University of Chicago Press, 2000), 720.

283. Moo, *The Letter to the Romans*, 111.

284. Johnson, "Paul and the Knowledge of God," 65.

285. Boa and Kruidenier, *Romans*, 62.

286. Moo, *The Letter to the Romans*, 120-122.

287. Ibid., 112.

288. Stott, *The Message of Romans*, 75.

Ungodliness/unrighteousness (motif B2) means *what* in 1:18? Paul declares God's wrath is against two primary human behaviors: ungodliness (*asebeia*), which BDAG indicates refers vertically to "a lack of reverence for deity and hallowed institutions as displayed in sacrilegious words and deeds" and may be translated "impiety;" and unrighteousness (*adikia*, occurring twice in 1:18), which BDAG indicates refers horizontally to "the quality of injustice" and may be translated "unrighteousness, wickedness, injustice."[289] Of the 1:18 ungodliness and unrighteousness, Stott asserts, "the first precedes and entails the second."[290] Lloyd-Jones wisely points out that ungodliness is defiance of the first great commandment (godliness, to love God) and unrighteousness of the second (righteousness, to love people), and they also correspond to the first and second portions of Moses' Ten Commandments, with ungodliness the essence of sin.[291] This human deterioration process of 1:18-20 is "repeated with horrifying emphasis" in 1:21-31.[292] Johnson claims, "perversion in life stems from perversion in faith. ... 'Ungodliness' is a religious word and is best seen in the idolatry described later (cf. vv. 21-23). 'Unrighteousness' is a moral term and is best expounded by the immorality spelled out in verses 24-32."[293] This author concurs that this pattern recurs in Paul's further description of ungodliness/unrighteousness in 1:21-32: 1:21a starting with sins directly against God (did not honor/thank Him), 1:21b-23 continuing with sins indirectly against God (futile reasoning, darkened hearts, foolishness), and 1:24-32 continuing with God judging those sins by giving man

---

289. Bauer, *A Greek-English Lexicon of the New Testament and Other Early Christian Literature*, 20, 141.

290. Stott, *The Message of Romans*, 72.

291. David Martyn Lloyd-Jones, *Romans Chapter 1: The Gospel of God* (Edinburgh: Banner of Truth, 1985), https://search-ebscohost-com.ezproxy.regent.edu/login.aspx?direct=true&db=rfh&AN=ATLA0000102004&site=ehost-live, 353-354, 356.

292. Stott, *The Message of Romans*, 75.

293. Johnson, "Paul and the Knowledge of God," 62.

up to sins against their own bodies and against others (including 1:29-31's "vice list"). Some interpret slightly differently, with 1:21a's sins directly against God leading to the sins of both 1:21b-23 and 1:24-32; but the conclusion remains that ungodliness precedes unrighteousness. On the question of whether unrighteousness is primarily forensic (man is legally not in right standing with God) or moral (man's behaviors defy God's standards), Moo concludes that Paul's usage of righteousness is commonly forensic and not simply moral, though morality is sometimes included.[294] Romans 1 seems to emphasize both the not right legal standing with God and related immoral behavior.

Truth known to all from nature (motif C1) means what, in terms of *what is the content of this truth*, in 1:18-20? The critical truth set revealed in nature (universe and human nature) since the world's creation is the Creator God's existence, His nature, and every human's nature as His creature including moral accountability to live in right relationship with Him and people. Specific references for this motif include at least "truth" (v18, 25), "God" (v19, 21, 28), "His invisible *attributes, that is,* His eternal power and divine nature" (v20), "what has been made" (v20), and "ordinance of God, that those who practice such things are worthy of death" (1:32). The term truth (*aletheia*) in 1:18 (and 1:25) refers to "the content of what is true," here "especially of the content of Christianity as the ultimate truth"[295] (at least to some of Christianity's content). That which is "known about God" (v19) is explained as 1:20's "invisible *attributes*," which are further explained as "eternal power and his deity."[296] Rasmussen on Romans 1 notes that we can reason that power must have a source and came into existence in our

---

294. Moo, *The Letter to the Romans*, 82-100, esp. 94.

295. Bauer, *A Greek-English Lexicon of the New Testament and Other Early Christian Literature*, 42.

296. Moo, *The Letter to the Romans*, 115.

universe on its own, and therefore is a *necessarily existent* power.[297] (This correlates with natural theology's cosmological argument.) This "eternal power" "is specific and suggests his omnipotence, as well as implying His eternity," and "His invisible *attributes*" "refers to the sum of divine attributes, or His Godhood;" thus they "suggest a full revelation of the being, the majesty and the glory of God," according to Johnson.[298] "Divine nature" or divinity (*theiotes*) in v20 means "the quality or characteristic(s) pertaining to deity."[299] But becoming aware of one's Creator God and these attributes also causes awareness of one's responsibility as His creature. Moo observes, "'truth' in the NT is not simply something to which one must give mental assent; it is something to be done, to be obeyed."[300] Bruce says the 1:18 truth includes "enough of His nature to prevent [one] from the error of identifying any of the created things with the Creator, enabling him to keep his conception of the Deity free from idolatry."[301] Boa and Kruidenier indicate that idolatry, such as in 1:21-23, should be understood by humanity as sin because "only two categories of 'entities' exist in the biblical universe: Creator and created. And these two are separated by an infinite gulf of worth, or glory."[302] "There is enough in creation and providence and history to establish the fact that God is the Creator and that God is the moral governor of this universe," asserts Lloyd-Jones.[303] Seifrid explains that this general revelation gives knowledge of both God and His will, as confirmed in 1:32 on the "ordinance of God" pronouncing death to

---

297. Rasmussen, *How Reason Can Lead to God*, 57-58.

298. Johnson, "Paul and the Knowledge of God," 69.

299. Bauer, *A Greek-English Lexicon of the New Testament and Other Early Christian Literature*, 446.

300. Moo, *The Letter to the Romans*, 114.

301. Bruce, *Romans*, 91.

302. Boa and Kruidenier, *Romans*, 51-52.

303. Lloyd-Jones, *Romans Chapter 1: The Gospel of God*, 374.

those practicing unrighteousness.[304] Here "ordinance" (*dikaioma*) means "a regulation relating to just or right action" and can be translated regulation, requirement, or commandment.[305] Moo points out, "v. 32 strongly implies that some knowledge of God remains even after a person has fallen into the degenerate state that Paul depicts in these verses."[306] Rowland asserts that Scripture uses "appeals to nature as the teacher of right conduct, a form of argument which has been central to much natural theology," with an example in "natural" relations of 1:26.[307] Haines argues that the Church traditionally believes Romans 2:14-15, which references the human heart, conscience, and thoughts (mind), says pagans, "without divinely inspired Scriptures, are able both (1) to know that God exists and that there is a divine law, and (2) to consciously seek to obey it – sometimes successfully, sometimes not."[308] Dunn identifies "the interplay in Jewish wisdom between the hiddenness and revelation of divine wisdom (see particularly Job 28 …)" as relevant to Paul's thought about the known truth.[309] "This knowledge is both limited and impure; it is confined to those basic attributes of God that may be discerned in nature (v. 20) … Further, … the knowledge of God that people possess outside special revelation is woefully inadequate,

---

304. Mark A. Seifrid, "Natural Revelation and the Purpose of Law in Romans," *Tyndale Bulletin* 49, no. 1 (May 1998): 115–29, https://search-ebscohost-com.ezproxy.regent.edu/login.aspx?direct=true&db=rfh&AN=ATLA0000999137&site=ehost-live, 120.

305. Bauer, *A Greek-English Lexicon of the New Testament and Other Early Christian Literature*, 249.

306. Moo, *The Letter to the Romans*, 134.

307. Christopher Rowland, "Natural Theology and the Christian Bible," *The Oxford Handbook of Natural Theology*, Ed. Russell Re Manning (Oxford, U.K.: Oxford University Press, 2013), 26-27.

308. Haines, *Natural Theology*, 42-43.

309. James D. G. Dunn, *Word Biblical Commentary: Volume 38A, Romans 1-8* (Dallas: Word Books, 1988), https://search-ebscohost-com.ezproxy.regent.edu/login.aspx?direct=true&db=rfh&AN=ATLA0000118409&site=ehost-live, 57.

of itself, to save," observes Moo, but it does lead "to the demonstration that God's condemnation is just: people are 'without excuse.'"[310]

Having knowledge of truth known to all from nature (motif C2) means what, in terms of *how complete is this knowledge*, in 1:19-20? Paul uses terminology that leaves no doubt that he believes this truth is completely known to men, not known partially or as through a cloudy lens as some other truth may be. Such terminology includes: (1) v19's "known" (*gnostos*), meaning "pertaining to being able to being known" and translatable as "capable of being known" or "intelligible;"[311] (2) v19's "evident" (*phaneros*), meaning "pertaining to being evident so as to be readily known" and translatable as "visible, clear, plainly to be seen, open, plain, evident, known;"[312] (3) v20's "clearly perceived" (*kathorao*), translatable as "perceived" or "noticed" and can include an "inward seeing;"[313] and (4) v20's "understood" (*noeo*), meaning "to grasp or comprehend something on the basis of careful thought" and translatable as "perceive, apprehend, understand, gain an insight into."[314] Some say the "noetic" effects of sin preclude unbelievers from truly, completely knowing this truth to begin with; however, the related v20 term *noeo* and Paul's other terminology indicate that this truth is intelligible, visible, noticed, and apprehended. Stott concludes that "knowledge of God which is available to us through the natural order," while being inevitably limited to finite, fallen humanity, "is nevertheless *plain* or open."[315] Horne correctly claims that 1:20 "indicates that in certain respects even the unregenerate man

---

310. Moo, *The Letter to the Romans*, 117, 133.

311. Bauer, *A Greek-English Lexicon of the New Testament and Other Early Christian Literature*, 204.

312. Ibid., 1047.

313. Ibid., 493.

314. Ibid., 674.

315. Stott, *The Message of Romans*, 72-73.

possesses an accurate knowledge of the true God. ... The unregenerate man knows *about* Him but he does not know Him personally."[316]

Having knowledge of truth known to all from nature (motif C2) means what, in terms of *how is this knowledge acquired*, in 1:19-20? While the text "does not tell us exactly by what means God makes himself known,"[317] Dunn wisely summarizes, "God's knowability is not merely a characteristic or 'spin-off' of creation but was willed and effected by God."[318] "God wants humankind to know him!," claim Boa and Kruidenier.[319] In v19 the verb "made evident" (*phaneroo*) means "to cause to become known" and is translatable as "disclose, show, make known."[320] God Himself causes it to happen through revelation. In explaining 1:19, Moo says, "what can be known of God has been made visible *because* God has 'made it known.' Only by an act of revelation from above – God 'making it known' – can people understand God as he is."[321] God's v20 making of "what has been made," which includes both what humans observe/perceive in all creation and their capabilities to do so, causes His general truth to be known, that is, reveals His truth to humans; this is what general revelation is. Stott asserts that "the creation is a visible disclosure of the invisible God, an intelligent disclosure of the otherwise unknown God. ... This truth of revelation through creation is a regular theme of Scripture."[322] Moo indicates that "the knowledge of God rejected by those depicted in 1:18-32 comes solely

---

316. Horne, "Toward a Biblical Apologetic," 90.

317. Groothuis, *Christian Apologetics* (2011), 178.

318. Dunn, *Romans 1-8*, 57.

319. Boa and Kruidenier, *Romans*, 48.

320. Bauer, *A Greek-English Lexicon of the New Testament and Other Early Christian Literature*, 1048.

321. Moo, *The Letter to the Romans*, 115.

322. Stott, *The Message of Romans*, 73.

through 'natural revelation' – the evidences of God in creation and, perhaps, the conscience."[323] Boa and Kruidenier claim, "That which God has made known to humanity is **his eternal power and divine nature**. That is the external part of his self-revelation. But in addition to demonstrating externally…, God has even caused man to understand internally what is seen externally,"[324] from general revelation's four sources of creation, history, man's moral thread, and man's religious nature.[325] "Although sin corrupts the whole person, it does not destroy the capacity to reason, nor does it have any effect on the objective standards of rationality," according to Hanna, for "without these standards remaining intact along with some capacity to reason, human life would not be possible. They are also essential for human responsibility."[326] Hanna also asserts, "Even when faith in God is absent, reason and conscience continue to testify to His reality (Romans 2:1-4, 14-15)."[327] Horne declares that the unbeliever has this knowledge, because "this knowledge is a logical deduction from the created universe rather than a personal encounter with Christ. … '… it is the seeing of understanding, of intelligent conception.'"[328]

Suppressing knowledge of truth known to all from nature (motif C3) means *what* in 1:18? This suppression is a holding down of that known truth and doing so "in unrighteousness." "Suppress" (*katecho*) in v18 means "to prevent the doing of something or cause to be ineffective" and more specifically in this case "hold down, suppress" or "stifle."[329] The root

---

323. Moo, *The Letter to the Romans*, 108.

324. Boa and Kruidenier, *Romans*, 50.

325. Ibid., 64.

326. Hanna, "What Is the Relationship Between Faith and Reason?," 54.

327. Ibid.

328. Horne, "Toward a Biblical Apologetic," 90.

329. Bauer, *A Greek-English Lexicon of the New Testament and Other Early Christian Literature*, 532.

segments of *katecho* mean down and have/hold, further confirming its meaning as to have/hold something but keep it down/back/fast so it cannot be useful or go anywhere. Boa and Kruidenier highlight Barrett's translation of 1:18 using *"hold imprisoned"* instead of "suppress,"[330] noting that "the suppression is not accidental; rather, it is very much intentional" as evidenced by the Greek *katecho* meaning "to hold fast, firmly" or to "restrain."[331] Humans suppress truth knowledge "in unrighteousness," which could mean this suppression is an act of unrighteousness or, more likely, their current unrighteousness provokes the suppression because they desire to continue in that unrighteousness. Stott argues that humans "have made an *a priori* decision to live for themselves, rather than for God and others, and therefore, deliberately stifle any truth which challenges their self-centeredness."[332] Bruce states, "the knowledge of the true God was accessible, but men and women closed their minds to it;" "it is a deliberate ignorance."[333] Sin's effects "[incite] humans to suppress awareness" of God's reality and ultimacy, according to Hanna, and further, "the sinful desire for complete autonomy is at the root of mankind's attempt to entirely eliminate the thought of God from their minds (Romans 1:28)."[334]

Accountability for suppressing knowledge of truth known to all from nature (motif C4) means *what* in 1:20? "Without excuse" (*anapologetos*) in v20 means "without excuse, inexcusable,"[335] or without a defense (in contrast to idea in 2:15's "thoughts alternately accusing or else defending them" where defending is verb *apologomai*). Haines quotes Hodge as saying,

---

330. Boa and Kruidenier, *Romans*, 48.

331. Ibid., 49.

332. Stott, *The Message of Romans*, 72.

333. Bruce, *Romans*, 89.

334. Hanna, "What Is the Relationship Between Faith and Reason?," 54.

335. Bauer, *A Greek-English Lexicon of the New Testament and Other Early Christian Literature*, 71.

"both in reference to his own nature and to the rule of duty, he has, in his works and in the human heart, given sufficient light to render the impiety and immorality of men inexcusable, vers. 19, 20, 32."[336] Seifrid points out that Paul uses the same term "without excuse" in both 1:20 and 2:1.[337] 2:1 indicates that those judging others by moral law yet practicing "the same things" as those described by the idolatry of 1:21-32 remain without excuse. Further, Seifrid points out that in 2:14f Paul is saying that "the created order ... supplies an equivalent internal witness" as the law to the gentiles, so both Jew and gentile are similarly accountable,[338] with "their thoughts alternately accusing or defending them" (2:15). Paul ends his 1:18-3:20 explanation of man's unrighteousness problem with another accountability decree in 3:19-20, stating, "... whatever the Law says, it speaks ... so that ... all the world may become accountable to God; because by the works of the Law none of mankind will be justified in His sight; for through the Law *comes* knowledge of sin." Of human accountability, Johnson concludes that Paul's assertion is that since man's fall, general revelation's purpose is "simply the negative purpose and function of preserving man's responsibility before God, because it heightens the conviction of sin and brings to consciousness the state of inexcusability."[339] Thus, general revelation purposes, amongst other things, to point humans toward the need for God and His gospel.

Summary of Romans 1:18-20 Main Message and Objections

In Romans 1:18-20, Paul concisely summarizes the human unrighteousness problem with God: although God has revealed through nature sufficient knowledge of Himself and His

---

336. Haines, *Natural Theology*, 41.

337. Seifrid, "Natural Revelation and the Purpose of Law in Romans," 119.

338. Ibid., 122.

339. Johnson, "Paul and the Knowledge of God," 70-71.

expectations for humans to live righteously, humans have chosen to suppress that knowledge and live in ungodliness and unrighteousness, thus invoking His wrath. Paul's terminology is quite clear and quite condemnatory about this. This message is confirmed by his placement of it just prior to 1:21-3:20's detailed focus on universal human ungodliness and unrighteousness and accountability to God, and further by his placement of 1:18-3:20 between his 1:16-17 gospel summary and his 3:21-4:25 explanation of the gospel's essence of salvation through righteousness by faith in Christ's works alone.

This main message of 1:18-20 might be restated within the following questions and answers that highlight the main motifs:

- The gospel (as 1:16-17 summarizes) is the solution to what primary problem?
  God's wrath on humans (A).
- God's wrath is the result of what primary human conditions?
  Ungodliness and unrighteousness (B2).
- This human ungodliness/unrighteousness occurs primarily for what reason?
  The suppression of God's truth while choosing unrighteousness (C3).
- Do humans clearly know this truth?
  Yes, because God made it clearly known to all humans (C2).
- What is this truth that is known yet being suppressed?
  Truth known from nature about God and His expectations for living (C1).
- Are humans truly accountable to God for ungodliness and unrighteousness?
  Yes, for the reasons discussed, humans are without excuse (C4).

Some commentators object in minor ways to this author's depiction of the main message of not only 1:18-20 but also of 1:18-3:20. They include Boa and Kruidenier, who assert that people are under God's wrath for different reasons: Gentiles because they suppress general revelation and Jews because they live contrary to special revelation in God's Law to them.[340] While acknowledging that unrepentant Gentiles and Jews will be judged differently, I disagree with that assertion as stated because it infers that those who trust in works of the Law for

---

340. Boa and Kruidenier, *Romans*, 46.

salvation correctly understand general revelation and have not suppressed aspects of it (such as evil in them causing judgment) leading to trust in their works.

Certain objectors to natural theology claim that Romans 1:18-3:20 argues or implies natural theology argumentation should not be used by believers. One objector to natural theology due to noetic sin effects, Moore, says Paul implies in 1:18ff that "Christians should avoid [antecedent natural theology]," which he defines as requiring "Christian beliefs to be rationally warranted."[341] Another objector, Horne, correctly indicates that general revelation suppression in Romans 1 is condemnatory, but continues without convincing evidence to an incorrect conclusion that general revelation is solely condemnatory and "there can be no ground for a natural theology in a consistently Biblical apologetic."[342] Yet another objector, Dennison, totally rejects the common understanding of 1:18-20 by asserting that Paul says God is making something evident not by what humans observe in the created order but by what humans observe in the history of that order, which includes special revelation of the Son; thus for Dennison there is no general revelation.[343] Some objectors, including presuppositionalists such as Spencer, believe not only that the "knowledge" of 1:18-20 is a lower form of knowledge, but also and without cause that all reasoning with unbelievers must assume they are closed-minded toward Him.[344]

---

341. Andrew Moore, "Should Christians do Natural Theology," *Scottish Journal of Theology* 63, no. 2 (2010): 127–45, https://search-ebscohost-com.ezproxy.regent.edu/login.aspx?direct=true&db=rfh&AN=ATLA0001784070&site=ehost-live, 127, 134.

342. Horne, "Toward a Biblical Apologetic," 90.

343. Dennison, "Natural and Special Revelation: A Reassessment," 30, 33-34.

344. Stephen R. Spencer, "Is Natural Theology Biblical?," *Grace Theological Journal* 9 (Spr 1988): 59–72, https://search-ebscohost-com.ezproxy.regent.edu/login.aspx?direct=true&db=rfh&AN=ATLA0000803112&site=ehost-live, 70-72.

Paul specifies that the suppression of general revelation knowledge, including some form of natural theology logic that humans can discern, provides sufficient cause for God to judge human unrighteousness. Stott says Paul is saying that "through general revelation people can know God's power, deity and glory (not his saving grace through Christ), and that this knowledge is enough not to save them but rather to condemn them, because they do not live up to it."[345] Thus, the special revelation of righteousness through faith in Christ's works is needed for salvation. Paul's purpose for 1:18-32 is to "show that the whole of humanity is morally bankrupt, unable to claim a favourable verdict at the judgment bar of God, desperately in need of his mercy and pardon."[346] Dunn asserts that Paul's "resolution is that the effect of divine wrath upon man is to show that man who rebels against his relation of creaturely dependence on God (which is what faith is) becomes subject to degenerative processes. Deliverance from these comes through returning to the relation of faith."[347]

Salvation is God's goal for unbelievers, but are natural theology arguments from general revelation potentially useful to help unbelievers see their need for salvation? General revelation truth includes not only God's greatness revealed in creation of the universe and human nature, but also, as described in Romans 1:18-3:20, the truth and condemnatory impact of humanity's ungodliness and unrighteousness. This author believes that if unbelievers are not responsive to solely special revelation arguments about salvation through righteousness by faith in Christ's works, then natural theology arguments are valid potential tools to help them first understand the truth of the Theistic God from general revelation. In such cases this general revelation may help

---

345. Stott, *The Message of Romans*, 74.

346. Bruce, *Romans*, 88.

347. Dunn, *Romans 1-8*, 55.

an unbeliever *un-suppress* the truth about God and themselves, and thereby see their need for God's salvation through special revelation.

Natural Theology's Apologetic Use by Paul in Acts

Acts 14 and 17 record dialogue by Paul (and Barnabas) using natural theology apologetic arguments which are consistent with Romans 1:18-20's accountability of man to God. Most substantial dialogue of Paul in Acts reveals interactions with Jews or with gentiles in authority with whom he is defending his Judaism against accusations by Jews; therefore, because in those cases theism is assumed, natural theology arguments are unnecessary. But Acts 14 and 17 are dialogue passages that reason with gentiles not judging his Judaism. Pearcey comments that when addressing Jews "the apostles could simply lay out their arguments why Jesus fit the criteria for the expected Messiah. By contrast, when addressing an audience of gentiles, who had no background knowledge of the Hebrew Scripture, the apostles had to begin at a much more fundamental level."[348] Haines highlights an observation by Bruce, "pagans must first be taught what Jews already confess regarding the unity and character of God."[349]

Paul's dialogues with gentiles in Acts 14 and 17 contain similar natural theology arguments. Similar propositions in both chapters include that nature reveals one living God who is Creator, Ruler, and Provider and is to be worshipped. (Only Acts 17 dialogue clearly contains an argument from special revelation, that Jesus' resurrection is proof that God is Judge.) Chan's analysis focuses on natural theology's "common ground" for this gentile evangelism, saying, "the apostles look for common ground in God's common grace (sending rain, making crops

---

348. Nancy Pearcey, "Foreword," *The Story of Reality: How the World Began, How It Ends, and Everything Important That Happens in Between,* by Gregory Koukl, 13-16 (Grand Rapids, MI: Zondervan, 2017), 14.

349. Haines, *Natural Theology*, quoting Bruce, 30-31.

grow, providing food), general revelation (his creation), and the universal human desire to worship a god."[350]

Acts 14 Natural Theology

When Paul and Barnabas' ministry in Lystra results in a significant healing followed by many beginning to treat them as gods, they employ natural theology arguments to attempt to stop this treatment and turn the people toward God (Acts 14:8-18, esp. 15-17). "The indigenous residents of Lystra were rural, and rural interests in Asia Minor diverged sharply from those of urban communities," according to Keener, "Paul thus appeals to God's testimony in rains and fruitful seasons … God's benevolence."[351] Keener further states that this preaching is "intelligible to a pagan audience."[352] Stott similarly observes that this is Paul's "only recorded address to illiterate pagans. … with the pagans in Lystra he focused not on a Scripture they did not know, but on the natural world around them, which they did know and could see."[353] "Even a brief survey of important commentaries on the Book of Acts reveals that the Church has traditionally understood these verses to contain an explicit appeal to natural revelation and the ability of unregenerate humans to understand," asserts Haines.[354]

Acts 17 Natural Theology

When Paul's conversations with and preaching of Jesus to Greek philosophers in Athens results in them taking Paul to the Areopagus so Paul could further discuss this with those

---

350. Chan, *Evangelism in a Skeptical World*, 67.

351. Craig S. Keener, *Acts,* New Cambridge Bible Commentary (Cambridge, UK: Cambridge University Press, 2020), 355.

352. Ibid., 353.

353. John R. W. Stott, *The Message of Acts: To the Ends of the Earth, Revised Ed.,* The Bible Speaks Today (Downers Grove, Ill.: InterVarsity Press, 2020), 212.

354. Haines, *Natural Theology*, 33.

gathered, Paul employs natural theology arguments as part of his message (Acts 17:16-34, esp. 22-31). Groothuis declares this is "the most detailed account in Acts of a Christian teacher challenging non-Jewish thinkers."[355] This message "has been traditionally used as an example of Paul's use of natural theology in interaction with a pagan audience."[356]

Some authors assert wisely that Paul challenged both main philosophies of this literate gentile audience: Epicureanism and Stoicism. Groothuis observes,

> Paul begins ... with ... the biblical doctrine of creation – a belief alien to both Stoics and Epicureans ... The Stoics believed in an impersonal 'world soul' – something like today's New Age spiritual principle ... – while the Epicureans believed in several deities who had no interest in humanity. This Creator, Paul declares, is also closely involved with humanity. ... Against the Athenian philosophies, Paul presents a God who is personal, transcendent, immanent and relational.[357]

Paul "does not take for granted that [his hearers] accept the truth of basic monotheism, and that he can therefore preach the Gospel," asserts Haines.[358] Calvin's view is that Paul "begins by preaching basic monotheism and proposing to reveal the one true God who is worthy of worship."[359]

Paul's Areopagus preaching content provides consistency with Scripture, common ground with the audience, and comprehensiveness in covering general revelation's Creator worldview and special revelation's gospel call to repentance. On Paul's general revelation consistency, Keener claims Paul "follows biblical precedent" by making various points

---

355. Groothuis, *Christian Apologetics* (2011), 34.

356. Haines, *Natural Theology*, 33.

357. Groothuis, *Christian Apologetics* (2011), 35.

358. Haines, *Natural Theology*, 34.

359. Ibid., speaking of Calvin.

consistent with Genesis but with general revelation rather than Scripture quotation.[360] Paul establishes common ground with general revelation from both nature and quotes from Greek poets known to hearers. Stott highlights Paul's "comprehensiveness" in proclamation of "God in his fulness as Creator, Sustainer, Ruler, Father and Judge. ... He argued ... by natural or general revelation, and that their ignorance and idolatry are therefore inexcusable. So he called on them ... to repent. Now all of this is part of the gospel. Or at least it is the indispensable background."[361]

Natural Theology's Relevance Exemplified in Other Scripture Passages

Beyond Romans 1 and Acts 14/17, other passages use natural theology apologetic arguments which are consistent with Romans 1:18-20's accountability of man to God. Some reference natural theology argumentation directly, asking the audience to reason clear conclusions from nature, while others reference it indirectly, assuming the audience should be aware of certain conclusions. This section describes significant usage in Job and additional passages indicating general revelation through the universe and through human nature.

Job's Natural Theology

The Book of Job contains natural theology arguments made both by men to each other and by God to Job (with God's words also being special revelation). Ross asserts, "No other Bible book makes a stronger argument for God's revelation of himself to all humanity through nature's record."[362] Because this book is the first Scripture recorded, being prior to Moses' Pentateuch, these men have no special revelation at least through chapter 37. Most commentators

---

360. Keener, *Acts*, 443.

361. Stott, *The Message of Acts*, 273-274.

362. Hugh Ross, *Hidden Treasures in the Book of Job: How the Oldest Book in the Bible Answers Today's Scientific Questions (Reasons to Believe)* (Grand Rapids, MI: Baker Books, 2011), 83.

focus on the theology of suffering, as they should. However, within theological arguments in Job natural theology plays a role, both in chapters 3-37, where "neither Job nor his friends expressed even the slightest doubt about God's existence or his attributes of omnipotence, omniscience, and omnipresence,"[363] and in chapters 38-42, where God exhorts from nature lessons.

Chapters 3-37 reveal the firm belief in general revelation of the five men (Job, three friends, and Elihu) who discuss the cause of Job's great suffering (prior to God speaking). Ross identifies verses in Job chapters 5, 7, 9, 10, 11, 12, 25, 26, 28, 34, 36, and 37 in which the five proclaim things known about God from nature.[364] Job emphasizes one argument saying, "just ask the animals, and have them teach you; and the birds … Or speak to the earth … And … the fish" (12:7-8). "Job is loaded with powerful apologetics tools," says Ross, "God's creation miracles seemed obvious" and "little clouded [Job's] capacity to see the great spiritual truths God had revealed to all people through nature's record."[365] The five knew God as the cause of life's physical, soulish, and spiritual aspects.[366] While four of the five were later rebuked by God for certain untruths, that does not discount the truths they spoke. Exemplifying this, Job discerned "God's redemptive plan," according to Ross, who delineates it with references from chapters 9 to 23: my Creator exists, has limitless power and wisdom, cares for me, is good with His perfection standard; I fall short; He has a redemption plan; I must entrust self to Redeemer for rescue; if I do, rescue is assured; and if I don't, my condemnation is assured.[367]

---

363. Ibid., 110.
364. Ibid., 83.
365. Ibid., 13, 86.
366. Ibid., 128.
367. Ibid., 206-207.

Chapters 38-42 reveal God speaking lessons from nature (which might be considered both general and special revelation), which apparently Job's pride had kept him from learning previously from general revelation. God declares through nature's examples His greatness in power and wisdom compared to Job's comparative non-existent power and wisdom. God rebuked Job with lessons from:

38:1-38 – general creation
38:39-39:30 – ten creatures
40:1-14 – Job's limits and pride
40:15-41:34 – two scary creatures

Atkinson sees God as saying, "Here, in your world, Job, are inexplicable, unfathomable and fearful mysteries … God is all-knowing, all-powerful *and* all-good;"[368] therefore, "Job can rest secure, and live with his questions being unanswered."[369] In discussing God's teaching through twelve soulish creatures, Ross observes, "most humans today live too far from nature to notice the evidence, to 'ask the animals' or be taught by them."[370] Some commentators use God's rebuke of Job and three others to argue against natural theology. But this is not warranted because God's rebuke shows that they had insufficient general revelation, not that having general revelation is useless or harmful.

Through the Universe

Some additional Scripture passages either point out that God "speaks" through the universe or asks the audience to observe it and reason important conclusions about God and/or man. God's universe "speech" comes through nature (the physical and life forms with soul/spirit)

---

368. David Atkinson, *The Message of Job: Suffering and Grace, Revised Ed.*, The Bible Speaks Today (Downers Grove, IL: InterVarsity Press, 2022), 97-99.

369. Ibid., 101-102.

370. Ross, *Hidden Treasures in the Book of Job*, 168.

and through history. This section summarizes general revelation usage in Psalms 19, 8, 104, Matthew 6, and other passages, and discusses a related objection to natural theology.

Some commentators deny natural theology within passages about God revealing truth through nature, saying either the authors are not attempting to evangelize or are speaking special revelation only (by virtue of it being Scripture). For example, Spencer argues that while the nature Psalms (e.g., 8, 19, 29, 65, 104) are said by natural theologians to "speak of the revelation of God by that which he made, sustains, and governs," he believes natural theology is not supported primarily because the audience is not unredeemed and the psalmists are not attempting to evangelize.[371] This argument does not hold up because Psalms' audience is not intended to be solely the unredeemed, the unredeemed are not natural theology's sole audience, and evangelism is not its sole purpose.

Psalm 19 has two main parts, the first (vss. 1-6) indicating that the heavens and their expanse continuously speak to the earth of God's glory and work. 19:1 proclaims, "the heavens tell of the glory of God." Barr identifies "the emphasis in the first part on the *universality* of the heavenly speech. ... all this linguistic interchange – is like a tent for the sun ... As everyone on earth receives the heat of the sun, we are entitled to conclude, so everyone on earth receives the language of the heavens or some impression of it."[372] "Any willing hearer can get the message," concludes Wilcox.[373]

---

371. Spencer, "Is Natural Theology Biblical?," 59-72, esp. 67.

372. James Barr, *Biblical Faith and Natural Theology: The Gifford Lectures for 1991 Delivered in the University of Edinburgh* (New York, NY: Oxford University Press (Clarendon Press), 1993), 87-88.

373. Michael Wilcock, *The Message of Psalms 1-72: Songs for the People of God*, The Bible Speaks Today (Downers Grove, IL: InterVarsity Press, 2001), 71.

Psalm 8 expresses how considering God's greatness in creation we reason how awesome is his care for man. 8:1, 3 proclaim, "How majestic is Your name in all the earth, You who have displayed Your splendor above the heavens! ... When I consider Your heavens, the work of Your fingers ... What is man that you think of him." Frame observes, "One of the most obvious testimonies to God in the natural world is the sheer size of it all. ... indescribably great ... greatness is a palpable mark of God. ... That wonder at the sheer greatness of it all is one of the roots of religion."[374]

Psalm 104 praises God for His greatness and wisdom in creating many features of the earth and in its provision for inhabitants. 104:24 summarizes, "how many are Your works! In wisdom You have made them all." This psalm is "a celebration of the world and of God as its sustainer, more its sustainer than its creator," according to Barr, who adds that its features characteristic of natural theology include that "the poem starts from God and sees the world as from God's side ... there is no specific content that comes from [special] revelation."[375] Further, he asserts, "No other biblical passage so strongly emphasizes that it was the beneficent effects of divine sustenance for animals and for humanity that signified the nature of God."[376]

Matthew 6:25-34 (Luke 12 similar) depicts Jesus appealing to a natural theology argument from nature about God's goodness toward man, by asking hearers to consider something evident in nature then reason God's goodness so they can believe God for provision. He says "look at" birds being provided food/drink by God and reason, due to man's greater value to God than birds, that God provides food/drink for man regardless of worry. Further, He says

---

374. Frame, *Nature's Case for God*, 21, 25.

375. Barr, *Biblical Faith and Natural Theology*, 81-83.

376. Ibid., 84-85.

"notice" lilies being provided nice clothing by God and reason, again due to human value, that God similarly provides clothing.

Other passages, upon considering nature or history, declare God's attributes to be excellent. Some passages even intermix observation of God's work in nature and history, with examples being Psalm 136 (showing God's faithfulness) and Psalm 97 (showing God's righteousness). Some prophetic warnings condemn nations based on a people generally not considering what is observable and therefore not following God. Within Isaiah 40:12-31's argument that God is just to Israel, Isaiah reminds (vs. 26), "see who created these *stars*." Isaiah 5:11-16 declares that because some of God's people "do not pay attention to the deeds of the LORD, Nor do they consider the work of His hands, Therefore My people go into exile for their lack of knowledge." In other words, people should be reasoning from God's observable deeds and works; these two terms used elsewhere in the OT sometimes mean His deeds in human history and sometimes His deeds in creating nature.

Through Human Nature

Some additional Scripture passages suggest that God "speaks" through human nature in ways that expect all men to draw the same conclusions about God and man. God's human nature "speech" comes through awareness and use of human capacities such as morality (good vs. evil), wisdom (wise vs. foolish), and reason. For example, one conclusion is that God must have similar personal capacities (except without evil/sin). This section discusses general revelation related to morality (Psalm 19, 119, "natural" things passages), wisdom (Proverbs, Matthew 18), and reason.

Morality is based on a God-given human capacity, not on a set of recorded law, not even biblical law. "The biblical laws, however absolute in themselves, had some grounding in knowable principles: they were not totally and absolutely arbitrary. The biblical laws, though given by revelation, could be seen to be in accord with reason of some kind. ... they accorded with some sort of universal principles," according to Barr.[377] Thus, passages promoting God's general moral law (not national or priestly law) remind man of what God has spoken through human nature.

Specifics of God's moral law in Scripture may certainly be considered special revelation by being recorded there; however, general discussion of that law in Scripture suggests it is also intended as natural theology conclusions. For example, Psalm 19's second main part (vss. 7-14) declares God's "law"/testimony is good and has good effects. Many commentators, including Haines, see this "law" as special revelation.[378] Barr acknowledges this possibility, but observes, "the poem says nothing about the Law of Moses. ... the text does not require it. It is possible to read the text in another way, taking these as general terms for divine 'instruction' ... such instruction is likely to be universally available ... like the instruction of the Wisdom literature ... Taken this way, it definitely looks positively towards something like natural theology."[379] Wilcock says of this second part, "here ... 'law' is a wonderfully comprehensive word, meaning all that God wants us to know about himself. There is no life for the soul without that."[380] Psalm 119 concentrates on God's "law"/testimony in a manner similar to Psalm 19's second part. "Surprisingly, the classic elements of divine revelation to Israel are not mentioned at all ... specific commands to be followed ... are simply not mentioned," Barr states, "... the 'word' of

---

377. Ibid., 98, 100.

378. Haines, *Natural Theology*, 27.

379. Barr, *Biblical Faith and Natural Theology*, 87-88.

380. Wilcock, *The Message of Psalms 1-72*, 71-72.

God is something set up in the heavens: 'For ever ... thy word is set up in the heavens ... (vv. 89ff.).' ... 'In other words, the commandments ... constitute a kind of revealed natural law.'"[381] Elsewhere in Scripture, the term "natural" sometimes implies that humans know from nature what God commands, such as Romans 1:26-27 which specifies that not observing "natural relations" between a man and woman is unrighteousness.

Wisdom is based on a God-given human capacity, whereby the wise learn how to live successfully and fools "despise wisdom and instruction" (1:7). Proverbs frequently contrasts the wise with the fool, who Haines and Frankford characterize as "one who has refused to learn what he could have learned from observing the world,"[382] suggesting at least some wisdom is from general revelation. Rowland says, "Observation of nature, along with observations of humans relating, the pitfalls and advantages of different patterns of behaviour, offer a paradigm for understanding providence and what makes for the providential ordering of the world and people in it. ... particularly evident in the Book of Proverbs."[383] Concerning such wisdom in morals, Collins says it teaches "limit" (human control is limited so be humble) and "order" (certain acts have necessary consequences).[384] For example, Prov. 8:15-16 says "all [rulers] who judge rightly" do so by wisdom, implying such wisdom comes through general revelation. Romans 13:1-4 confirms this, implying governing authorities know from general revelation what is good (to approve) and wrong (to punish).[385] As another example of wisdom that should be gained through general revelation, in Matt. 18:12-13 Jesus says considering a shepherd's will motivated

---

381. Barr, *Biblical Faith and Natural Theology*, 89-90.

382. Haines and Fulford, *Natural Law*, 65-66.

383. Rowland, "Natural Theology and the Christian Bible," 27-28.

384. Haines and Fulford, *Natural Law*, speaking of Collins, 65.

385. Ibid., 101.

by compassion to rescue one missing sheep of one hundred from perishing should cause believing God wills rescuing each person from perishing.

Reason/rationality is based on a God-given human capacity, pointing to God having the personal trait of reason, a function of the mind. Many passages acknowledge or promote the use of reason not only for life generally but also specifically for considering what God desires to reveal to us and others. Some include Isaiah 1:18, 1 Peter 3:15, and Jude 3. Further discussion on reason relative to general revelation exists in prior sections, including in "Pursuing Christian Worldview Truth through Reason and Faith."

CHAPTER 4: NATURAL THEOLOGY'S RELEVANCE TODAY

Prior discussion has included the foundations of natural theology from literature review and examination of relevant Scripture. Scripture makes clear the existence of general revelation of God's truth, including that He exists and expects man's accountability. Romans 1 specifies this, while other passages consider various aspects of it. Literature review makes clear that today's primary nontheistic worldviews contradict theism on core concepts, and that during Church history at least some of the Church has refuted competing worldviews with natural theology argumentation. Its arguments (not including ontological) might be summarized as:

- **Universe** – Reasoning from observation of the universe's existence/sustenance and its complex order, including absolute truths and provision for life, concludes existence of a God with theistic attributes as its cause and designer and accountability of man to Him.
- **Human Nature** – Reasoning from observation of human nature's existence and freedom in greatness and lowliness, including its immaterial features of rational mind, moral conscience, intentional will, perception of beauty, etc., concludes existence of a God with theistic attributes as personal creator and accountability of man to Him.

This chapter proceeds to proposing how natural theology might be utilized within three primary areas of church ministries today: evangelism, impacting culture, and developing believers' relationship with God. For evangelism, natural theology may help unbelievers to understand Christianity's theistic basis and how their own worldviews have deficiencies. For impacting culture, its use may help some to understand that theistic values have bases in reason and therefore have a right to be heard, along with those promoting them. For developing believers, natural theology use may help some to have a more confident faith and as a result have greater cultural impact and evangelism success. Note that the previous section on "Nontheistic Worldviews Today" contains relevant considerations for those ministries, especially for evangelism.

Authors who identify natural theology relevance in terms that correlate with all three ministries include Craig, Haines and Fulford, Ross, Groothuis, and Wolterstorff. Craig argues that the three tasks of relevance for classical apologetics are "evangelizing unbelievers," "shaping culture," and "strengthening believers."[386] Haines and Fulford, who focus on the moral argument, assert that natural law can be helpful in apologetics; in ethics, engagement with the world, and law and politics; and in church history perspective and exegesis.[387] The Church's lack of teaching on creation (and corresponding natural theology) has impacted our evangelistic mission, cultural impact in the scientific community, and development of believers due to foundational Christian doctrines being obscured, according to Ross.[388] Groothuis, a classical apologist, describes three gospel environments: proclamation; defense against opposition, including religious, cultural, and political; and communal manifestation.[389] Wolterstorff summarizes Aquinas' three natural theology purposes as for apologetic-polemic, for metaphysics (shared purpose with unbelievers), and for transmutation (believers changing).[390]

Use of natural theology by the three church ministries may seem challenging. Clear reasoning is needed. But natural theology use does not necessarily involve presenting formal philosophical proofs with lengthy proposition and conclusion statements, though it can. Rather, arguments should be communicated in manners amenable to the circumstance and audience, whether the learned and/or unlearned. For in Romans 1:18-20 Paul makes no distinction as to who is capable of knowing truth about God's existence and man's accountability.

---

386. Craig, *Reasonable Faith*, 15-23.

387. Haines and Fulford, *Natural Law*, 50.

388. Ross, *Hidden Treasures in the Book of Job*, 11-12.

389. Groothuis, *Truth Decay*, 162.

390. Wolterstorff, "The Migration of the Theistic Arguments," 78.

And as with every challenge, we must rely on God's Spirit, in this case to grant wisdom in communicating and to cause the un-suppression of theistic truth.

Natural Theology Use in Evangelism

In the Church's evangelism ministry, natural theology utilization may be helpful if an unbeliever does not have a theistic worldview, with consideration of at least the following: being personal, as in all apologetics; finding common ground for theistic discussion; and reasoning theistic truths in contrast with nontheistic beliefs. Classical apologetics, sometimes called the two-step approach, has two parts with the first reasoning theism (natural theology), for as Groothuis summarizes, "First, apologetics labors to present the Christian worldview. ... Second, apologetics should show that [repentant faith] makes sense because Christianity is true, rational, and ... 'attractive.'"[391] However, if the second part (evidential argument) is used first and unsuccessfully, one might need to then use the first part to address nontheistic worldview beliefs. Frame says, "The Bible itself speaks of natural revelation, and it presents that natural knowledge as a kind of prerequisite ... to saving knowledge."[392] Multiple authors reference Schaeffer's assertion that Christianity does not start with Jesus saves from sins but rather from in the beginning God created, including Pearcey, who says ignoring that God created is "a major reason the message of Christianity no longer makes sense to many people today."[393]

Some authors describe all classical apologetics as "pre-evangelism;" others use that term for natural theology only. "Apologetics is pre-evangelism," according to Geisler, for "it is done

---

391. Groothuis, *Christian Apologetics* (2011), 41.

392. Frame, *Nature's Case for God*, 7.

393. Pearcey, "Foreword," 13.

before evangelism *if needed* or when an objection or question is raised."[394] Ham calls natural theology use (especially on creation) "pioneer evangelism (or pre-evangelism)" because it plows ground so the gospel can be sown.[395] And to some, pre-evangelism can refer to discussion of the basis of objective truth and reason as a prerequisite to natural theology discussion.

Being Personal, as in All Apologetics

Those evangelizing should be concerned with being personal, whether communicating with one or many. "Apologetics ... means talking to people, individuals, not answering generic arguments that all persons in a class have in common," note Clark and Geisler, "it provides tools ... from which individual answers are shaped to meet particular needs of particular persons at their particular level."[396] It includes seeking to understand people's assumptions and meanings of terms, for apologetics must be "person-sensitive and culturally aware. Unbelievers come to the table with a variety of issues, misconceptions and values that need to be discerned," reminds Groothuis.[397]

Gentleness and humble persuasion contribute to our message's plausibility (possibility of being true). Baggett and Baggett reiterate Horner's focus on gentleness for plausibility, commenting, "If someone, for whatever reason, doesn't think Christianity is even possibly true, then no number of credible reasons to believe will have much effect. ... doing apologetics in the

---

394. Normal L. Geisler, "What Is Apologetics and Why Do We Need It?," *The Comprehensive Guide to Apologetics*. Ed. Joseph M. Holden (Eugene, OR: Harvest House Publishers, 2018), 22.

395. Ken Ham, *Why Won't They Listen: The Power of Creation Evangelism* (Green Forest, AR: New Leaf Publishing (Master Books), 2002), 61.

396. Boa and Bowman, *Faith Has Its Reasons*, quoting Clark and Geisler's *Apologetics in the New Age*, pp. 226-227, 455.

397. Groothuis, *Truth Decay*, 184.

right way – with kindness, gentleness, winsomeness – can help render the gospel plausible."[398] Depoe highlights persuasive skills, stating, "The work of apologetics is not only to win arguments but to minister to the lost. Consequently, apologists would do well to develop a broader range of persuasive skills than logical argument by itself."[399] Craig reminds to humbly answer questions and let hearers make their own decisions with God, without "challenging [them] to 'just have faith.' ... many non-Christians ... were turned off to the gospel by having their honest questions squelched and being told to just believe."[400] Further, Craig recommends, "We needn't claim that we can prove to the unbeliever that God exists. ... we should simply claim that ... 'the arguments make it rational that God exists.'"[401]

Chatraw's evangelistic approach focuses more than most on being personal, recommending that initial discussion and primary arguments (which are based on natural theology human nature arguments) address significant personal desires, because his approach "is about engaging the deepest aspirations of our secular friends and asking them to consider how the story of the gospel ... just may lead them to what their heart has been looking for all along."[402] He proposes that areas of essential personhood, not the universe (e.g., cosmological and teleological arguments), be the focus.[403] This may not be the best sole focus for persons concerned with the universe/science/origins, but seems reasonable for persons mostly concerned with aspects of their humanity.

---

398. Baggett and Baggett, *The Morals of the Story*, 4-5.

399. Depoe, "The Place of Autonomous Reason and Logic in Theology," 64.

400. Craig, *Reasonable Faith*, 59.

401. Ibid., 189.

402. Chatraw, *Telling a* Better *Story*, 7.

403. Ibid., 42.

Finding Common Ground for Theistic Discussion

Those evangelizing should be concerned with finding common ground with unbelievers, particularly related to theistic worldview. Unbelievers may have questions and desires that theism answers, and likely have values/truths in common with it. Groothuis says in Acts Paul "[builds] a bridge instead of erecting a wall. … we should try to discern and capitalize on points of contact with these other worldviews."[404] "We have to begin where people are, to find a point of contact with them," asserts Stott, who provides examples such as "what constitutes authentic humanness, the universal quest for transcendence, the hunger for love and community, the search for freedom or the longing for personal significance."[405]

We should seek to find those beliefs that unbelievers already possess that are in common with theism. Craig observes,

> No atheist or agnostic really lives consistently with his worldview. In some way he affirms meaning, value, or purpose without an adequate basis. It is our job to discover those areas … We need not attack his values themselves – for they are probably largely correct – but we may agree with him concerning them, and then point out only that he lacks any foundation for those values, whereas the Christian has a foundation … for the values he already possesses.[406]

Chatraw's apologetics approach includes starting by listening to the other person's social imagination, to learn "what can we affirm, and what do we need to challenge?," for "in Athens Paul … entered their social imagination and leveraged their cultural stories … He quotes pagan stories and affirms where Athenian thinking is correct."[407] Thus, common ground may include beliefs derived from one's music, literature, or other cultural influences. Chan recommends

---

404. Groothuis, *Christian Apologetics* (2011), 35.

405. Stott, *The Message of Acts*, 212-213.

406. Craig, *Reasonable Faith*, 86-87.

407. Chatraw, *Telling a Better Story*, 66.

seeking connections related to general revelation, common grace, the image of God, eternity in our hearts, sin, and analogies of redemption.[408]

If an unbeliever seems to reject the notion of knowable objective spiritual truth, as can be true especially of postmodernists, then the nature of such truth should be discussed. Related material exists in a previous section titled "Pursuing Knowledge of Christian Worldview Truth Through Faith and Reason." Kreeft and Tacelli assert that four different skeptical or subjective truth theories "make apologetics impossible:" no objective truth, no knowable truth, no objective religious truth, and no knowable objective religious truth; therefore, these must be identified and refuted first.[409] The first three are supersets of the fourth, for which "religious" could be replaced with "spiritual." Groothuis indicates that "postmodernist thought is so confused" about the nature of truth and life implications that much related communication may be needed, and that this is particularly true in the secular university.[410]

Reasoning Theistic Truths in Contrast with Nontheistic Beliefs

Those evangelizing should be concerned with reasoning how specific nontheistic beliefs of an unbeliever's worldview are inconsistent/unlivable and how theistic worldview truths in contrast to those beliefs provide consistency and livability. A previous section titled "Natural Theology's Major Arguments as Evidence for Theism" discusses major natural theology arguments. In summary they reason from observations of the universe and human nature to conclude at least that the Theistic God exists (created everything, has certain great attributes), which requires man as creature having an accountable relationship with God. As noted earlier,

---

408. Chan, *Evangelism in a Skeptical World*, 148-153.

409. Kreeft and Tacelli, *Handbook of Christian Apologetics*, 366-368.

410. Groothuis, *Truth Decay*, 274, 184.

although formal philosophical proofs might not be needed, concepts consistent with them are, in manners amenable to the circumstance and audience.

Evangelistic discussion should investigate how specific nontheistic beliefs of unbelievers' worldviews are inconsistent or unlivable, as Chatraw emphasizes.[411] That is, we should help the unbeliever understand their known and previously unknown nontheistic beliefs and have doubts about their logical conclusions. Whether unbelievers have analyzed their presuppositions or not, we should help reveal them, says Schaeffer.[412] This task may be more complex with those believing a mix of ideas from multiple worldviews. Nontheistic beliefs might include those about universe/man's history, including evolution for example, for as Koukl indicates, "every worldview has four elements. ... These four parts are called creation, fall, redemption, and restoration," or alternatively origins, problem, solution, and repair.[413] When considering the nature of one's origins beliefs, Koukl asks, do they believe the cause is some One (theism's God), some thing (nonpersonal), or no one and no thing?[414] An example of an inconsistent/unlivable belief is the postmodernist concept of no objective truth, because they live as if such truth does exist in such things as mathematical/scientific absolute truths, moral stances against murder and child harm, contracts, finances, their own reasoning, and even their "truth" that no truth exists.

With an unbeliever's primary nontheistic beliefs and their logical conclusions identified, evangelistic discussion should show how contrasting theistic truths provide an internally

---

411. Chatraw, *Telling a* Better *Story*, 54-70.

412. Schaeffer, *The Francis A. Schaeffer Trilogy*, 132.

413. Koukl, *The Story of Reality*, 25.

414. Ibid., 63.

consistent and livable worldview. Modernists might be more concerned with consistency, postmodernists and monists possibly with livability. Ham declares the most foundational truth, "if God is not Creator, then nothing else matters. All is meaningless."[415] Stott highlights Paul's "comprehensiveness" of truths in Acts 17 as our example, saying he proclaims "God in his fulness as Creator, Sustainer, Ruler, Father and Judge. ... He argued that human beings already know these things by natural or general revelation, and that their ignorance and idolatry are therefore inexcusable."[416] Pearcey on Acts 17 notes that Paul "builds his argument on what everyone can know about God through the created order. ... After making sure his Greek audience understands who God is, only then does Paul take them to the moral implications. ... We are guilty of breaking a cosmic law, and the proper response is to heal the breach – what the Bible calls repentance."[417]

Thus, natural theology may help unbelievers "unsuppress" the truth of God, helping them transition from nontheistic beliefs to realizing not only God and His amazing creation including man's personal attributes, but also their desperate need as creatures morally accountability to God (as Paul highlights in Romans 1:18-20), for which the Christian gospel is the only reasonable solution. Chan suggests that once moral accountability is realized, we find a redemptive analogy that makes sense relative to their existential cry, using it in a storyline with the gospel as the happy ending.[418]

---

415. Ham, *Why Won't They Listen?*, 100.

416. Stott, *The Message of Acts*, 273-274.

417. Pearcey, "Foreword," 14-15.

418. Chan, *Evangelism in a Skeptical World*, 148-153.

Natural Theology Use in Impacting Culture

In the Church's ministry of impacting culture, natural theology utilization may be helpful in at least two ways: impacting collective cultural thought toward reasonability of the gospel's theistic foundation and impacting specific cultural spheres toward increased truth and resulting good. Spheres (areas) of culture might be categorized as: family, education, business, government/law, science/technology, news/media, arts/entertainment/sports, religion, healthcare, etc. Some spheres will be discussed further; others will not.

Impacting Collective Thought Toward Theism's Reasonability

Culture's collective thought (its current narrative's primary ideas) sometimes accepts theistic truths but more often denies them. Chatraw observes how this has changed over time, saying, "At one time in the West, Christianity seemed plausible because elements of the Christian story were intentionally woven into the fabric of everyday life. ... At the very least, the belief in God – and more specifically the God of the Bible – seemed a viable option for most ... Now the cultural narratives that seep into our psyches have changed."[419] Groothuis emphasizes the ideas controlling cultural thought when quoting Machen saying, "false ideas are the greatest obstacles to the reception of the gospel" and arguing that evangelism will be relatively unsuccessful "if we permit the whole collective thought of the nation or of the world to be controlled by ideas which ... prevent Christianity from being regarded as anything more than a harmless delusion."[420]

The Church should use natural theology to impact culture's collective thought, not solely for the sake of theism's prominence, but for the sake of the gospel having greater opportunity

---

419. Chatraw, *Telling a Better Story*, 1.

420. Groothuis, *Christian Apologetics* (2011), 28.

due to its theistic foundation being rejected less frequently. Craig, who believes a primary task of natural theology is "shaping culture," correctly declares,

> Western culture is deeply post-Christian. ... Why are ... considerations of culture important? ... because the gospel is never heard in isolation. It is always heard against the background of the cultural milieu in which one lives. ... If the situation is not to degenerate further, it is imperative that we shape the intellectual climate of our nation ... It is the broader task of Christian apologetics to help create and sustain a cultural milieu in which the gospel can be heard as an intellectually viable option for thinking men and women. ... apologetics ... gives them ... intellectual permission to believe.[421]

Plantinga, similar to Craig, indicates that certain natural theology arguments are helpful to establish theism's "rational acceptability," which is "at least one of the aims" of natural theology.[422]

Impacting Cultural Spheres Toward Increased Truth/Good

While impacts of natural theology truths within specific cultural spheres can influence collective thought, those impacts also increase the truth and resulting good in the specific spheres. Haines and Fulford confirm Scripture's allowance for cultural engagement, "specifically of a kind that can admit goodness and value outside the visible church."[423] Gould wisely promotes "cultural apologetics" which, integrated with other apologetic approaches, is

> the *work of establishing the Christian voice, conscience, and imagination within a culture so that Christianity is seen as true and satisfying.* ... 'faithfully present within' culture ... Christians are called to be creators and cultivators of the good, true, and beautiful. ... The cultural apologist works to *resurrect relevance* ... and ... to *resurrect hope*, creating new cultural goods and rhythms and practices that reflect the truth, beauty, and goodness of Christianity.[424]

---

421. Craig, *Reasonable Faith*, 16-19.

422. Plantinga, "A Recent Modal Ontological Argument," 138.

423. Haines and Fulford, *Natural Law*, 108.

424. Gould, *Cultural Apologetics*, 21-24.

These "goods" occur within one or more specific cultural spheres. The following discussion focuses on science/technology, education, and government/law.

Today's cultural sphere of science/technology needs natural theology's influence. Craig asserts that, in science, engineering, and technology, people are "deeply modernist."[425] Previous sections, including the modernism worldview section, further discuss naturalism (only the physical exists, not God or soul), which encompasses evolution and other concepts. Evolutionary thinking is pervasive throughout culture, according to Ham, who emphasizes, "Creation vs. evolution is NOT a side issue. They are really the front lines of the battle."[426] Luskin and Meyer summarize the ongoing supposed historical conflict between science and religion, saying,

> in the decades following the publication of *Origin of Species* (1859), a 'warfare model' of science and religion became 'ingrained into the received wisdom of many secular Americans.' ... 'science' stood for freedom and progress against the superstition and repression of 'religion.' ... But this warfare model ... is fake history ... the founders of modern science were inspired to their scientific research *precisely because of their religious beliefs* ... it's because the Judeo-Christian worldview that permeated Western culture proposed that a rational, orderly, and moral-lawgiving God created a rational and orderly universe that was governed by predictable physical laws. Simultaneously ... the ... worldview taught that nature was not sacred, and thus could be studied and enjoyed ... even more, this worldview encouraged the humility necessary to admit mistakes and abandon wrong ideas.[427]

While Holder observes concerning recent history that "there is a flourishing dialogue between science and theology,"[428] the science/technology sphere is yet in great need of the truth and good that could result from natural theology influence.

---

425. Craig, *Reasonable Faith*, 16-19.

426. Ham, *Why Won't They Listen*, 80-81.

427. Casey Luskin and Stephen C. Meyer, "Has the Christian Worldview Had a Positive Impact on the Development of Science?," *The Comprehensive Guide to Apologetics*, Ed. Joseph M. Holden (Eugene, OR: Harvest House Publishers, 2018), 285-289.

428. Rodney D. Holder, "Natural Theology in the Twentieth Century," *The Oxford Handbook of Natural Theology*, Ed. Russell Re Manning (Oxford, U.K.: Oxford University Press, 2013), 131-132.

But how can natural theology be utilized to impact the science/technology sphere? Classical apologists believe we "should seek to show that Christianity is consistent with the scientific facts," while being cautious about the latest theories posed by scientists, according to Boa and Bowman.[429] Taliaferro argues that the Church, as it has opportunities within culture, should use natural theology's theistic arguments at a minimum to provide a real philosophical alternative to naturalism (theism's closest competitor), if not also to provide doubt in those who have previously accepted it without debate.[430] Polkinghorne highlights how natural theology addresses two critical meta-questions: *"Why is science possible at all?"* ("science is possible, and mathematics is so unreasonably effective, just because the universe is a creation and human beings are ... creatures made in the image of their Creator") and *"Why is the universe so special?"* (unique fine-tuning for life from its big bang beginning seems most probable as the result of natural theology's intelligent creator/designer explanation).[431] Ross emphasizes the value of providing reasonable answers, saying, "when skeptics and seekers receive thoughtful, reasonable answers to their questions about science, creation, evolution, and human behavior, they gain a desire to learn more about God and the possibility of developing a relationship with him."[432] But because much of the Church's withdrawal from teaching on creation and related topics "has crippled both the church and the scientific community," Ross argues for a focused

---

429. Boa and Bowman, *Faith Has Its Reasons*, 80.

430. Charles Taliaferro, "The Project of Natural Theology," *The Blackwell Companion to Natural Theology*, Eds. William Lane Craig and J. P. Moreland (Chichester, West Sussex, UK: Wiley-Blackwell, 2012), 2-3.

431. John Polkinghorne, "Where Is Natural Theology Today?," *Science & Christian Belief* 18, no. 2 (October 2006), https://search-ebscohost-com.ezproxy.regent.edu/login.aspx?direct=true&db=rlh&AN=22322057&site=ehost-live, 172-176.

432. Ross, *Hidden Treasures in the Book of Job*, 21.

academic "strategy of engagement. Christians … need to study science and engage with scientists at the highest academic and research levels."[433]

Today's cultural sphere of education also needs natural theology's influence. Universities and primary/secondary schools should be a Church focus for natural theology usage, not only in science/technology but in all departments. Eddy reminds that in the Western nineteenth century "primary school students were often instructed to observe the wisdom of God evinced in nature, and university students were taught … kinds of natural theology arguments."[434] Restoration of such instruction is desirable. "The single most important institution shaping Western culture is the university. … It is at the university that [future professionals] will formulate or, more likely, simply absorb the worldview that will shape their lives," observe Moreland and Craig, who propose, "If the Christian worldview can be restored to a place of prominence and respect at the university, it will have a leavening effect throughout society. If we change the university, we change our culture through those who shape culture."[435] Groothuis highlights the need to impact the anti-theistic bias in philosophy education, saying, "virtually all topical introductions to philosophy contain sections on the existence of God that quote or borrow extensively from Hume and his successors," who promote an anti-God empiricism with attacks on natural theology foundations.[436] DeWeese and Moreland remind of Malik's 1980 warning that "the greatest danger confronting American evangelical Christianity is the danger of anti-intellectualism."[437]

---

433. Ibid., 11-12.

434. Eddy, "Nineteenth-Century Natural Theology," 100.

435. Moreland and Craig, *Philosophical Foundations for a Christian Worldview, 2nd Ed.*, 3-6.

436. Sennett and Groothuis, "Introduction," *In Defense of Natural Theology*, 9-10.

437. DeWeese and Moreland, *Philosophy Made Slightly Less Difficult*, 198-199.

Education impacts a person's worldview, often for their lifetime; the Church should impact education with natural theology's theistic worldview truths.

The cultural sphere of government/law also needs natural theology influence. When government officials at any level do not operate according to a standard of good for all (including freedom and equal justice), which natural theology and especially its moral argument (natural law) promote, injustice to someone results. Government/law serves people's good by protecting good and controlling evil, otherwise it controls some good and protects some evil. Mauser declares,

> many of the founding fathers of the United States of America believed strongly in the natural moral law. … it can help us to make arguments about what is morally good independent of the Scriptures in alignment with the Scriptures. … Insofar as we can introduce this way of thinking into our society, we can start restoring justice to evil places and evil practices. … we are called upon to stand for justice and use all the tools God has given us, including natural law, to point people to truth, goodness, and beauty.[438]

Haines and Fulford note a special protection of observed natural law, which "frees up the civil magistrate to carry out his office apart from subordination to the clergy, since he is equipped to reason justly."[439] The Church should not seek to rule over government/law, but should impact it by communicating natural theology truths as needed to encourage it to serve people's good.

Natural Theology Use in Developing Believers' Relationship with God

In the Church's ministry of developing believers' relationship with God, commonly termed discipleship, natural theology utilization may be helpful in multiple ways. Natural theology as well as evidentialist arguments (the other part of classical apologetics) focus on the

---

438. Bernard James Mauser, "A Tale of Two Theories: Natural Law in Classical Theism and Presuppositionalism," *Without Excuse: Scripture, Reason, and Presuppositional Apologetics*, Ed. David Haines (Leesburg, VA: The Davenant Press, 2020), 293.

439. Haines and Fulford, *Natural Law*, 111.

mind/intellect. Development of both heart and mind are critical to a believers' growth in relationship with God. Generally, natural theology use in discipleship should strengthen the theistic beliefs of the believer, including providing a broader picture of the full set of Christian beliefs. Haines, considering the relative importance of natural theology, asks, "why does this matter?," and provides a response that includes, "natural theology provides us all at once with demonstrations of the existence of God, which have" these four benefits:

> *apologetic* value … and knowledge of what God is not …
> *theological* value – helping us better interpret the Scriptures when they talk about the nature of God, and bringing us to a greater appreciation of the majesty of the God we love, serve, and worship …
> *practical or existential* value – bringing us ever before the provident God who wisely governs His creation, and reassuring us that if He takes care of the flowers and the birds, He knows how to take care of us …
> *adorative* value, for we only truly worship God when it is the true God we worship. When we are confronted with these truths about God, we are compelled to fall to our knees in worship of the sovereign Creator who transcends our world and our understanding.[440]

The three subsections following discuss natural theology in the development of believers' relationship with God for the purposes of knowing God better, resolving doubts, and persevering; of confident preparation for evangelism and cultural impact; and of Scripture interpretation. Haines' values correlate to these three purposes in this way: his last two and some of his first values correlate to the first purpose set, his first to the second purpose set, and his second to the third purpose. A final subsection considers the responsibilities of church leaders in these purposes.

For Knowing God Better, Resolving Doubts, and Persevering

Natural theology usage can facilitate knowing God better, resolving doubts, and persevering. Concerning knowing God better, Aquinas sees a natural theology purpose of

---

440. Haines, *Natural Theology*, 184-185.

changing believers toward ultimate happiness by knowing more of God. Wolterstorff explains Aquinas' perspective:

> the believer, loving the truth he believes, 'thinks out and takes to heart whatever reasons he can find in support thereof' ... The enterprise of natural theology ... represents an *advance* for the believer ... toward ultimate felicity. Our ultimate happiness lies in 'seeing' truths about God. And when we ... manage to demonstrate some of the things that we unseeingly took on faith, so that now we 'see' them to be true, that is a step up the road toward felicity. ... So ... a transmutation project addressed to believers. ... a key component in the pursuit of the contemplative life.[441]

Concerning resolving doubts, apologetic reasoning (including natural theology's arguments) "fortifies believers in their faith, whether they are wrestling with doubts and questions or simply seeking a deeper grounding for their biblical beliefs," says Groothuis.[442] While Plantinga proposes that religious belief is basic and so can warrant belief without theistic arguments, he also argues that such arguments can have value in various ways, which include to "strengthen and confirm theistic belief. Not nearly all believers hold theistic belief in serene and uninterrupted certainty; most are at least occasionally subject to doubts," and to "increase the warrant of the theistic belief."[443] Chatraw, who promotes telling an integrated God-story about all of life that includes versions of various natural theology arguments from human nature, declares, "Christians are not immune from doubts ... helping each other believe also means being able to answer tough intellectual questions. Part of the authenticity of compelling communities is a regular digging into the questions behind the doubts we all struggle with."[444]

---

441. Wolterstorff, "The Migration of Theistic Arguments," 71-72.

442. Groothuis, *Christian Apologetics* (2011), 25.

443. Walls and Dougherty, "Introduction,", 3-4.

444. Chatraw, *Telling a* Better *Story*, 12-13.

Concerning persevering, apologetics use (including natural theology) to help believers to know God better and resolve intellectual doubts can reduce apostasy. Craig asserts, "Contemporary Christian worship tends to focus on fostering emotional intimacy with God. While this is a good thing, emotions will carry a person only so far, and then he's going to need something more substantive. Apologetics can help to provide some of that substance."[445] Gould warns,

> record numbers of Christians – especially those thirty-five and under – are leaving the church and abandoning belief in God and Jesus Christ. Why? ... Barna poll ... identified six reasons ... *every single reason involves a failure to engage the life of the mind and employ apologetics to answer people's questions. ... Our greatest need is to reintroduce believers to the value and practice of apologetics and to equip them to engage our culture's ideas in a winsome and intelligent way.*[446]

The object of Enfield's classic work on natural theology is "to impress the youthful mind with a deep and abiding sense of the existence and attributes of God ... to fix this great truth, at an early age," so they would not be allured from duty to God.[447] Natural theology provides one tool to help engage Christian minds and resolve questions, and thereby reduce apostasy.

For Confident Preparation for Evangelism and Impacting Culture

Natural theology usage can facilitate a believer's confident preparation for evangelism and cultural impact. Prior sections in this chapter discussed natural theology usage as part of these two tasks; however, this subsection focuses on the preparation of the individual believer for these tasks. In the context of suffering for righteousness, Peter says "but sanctify Christ as Lord in your hearts, always *being* ready to make a defense to everyone who asks you to give an

---

445. Craig, *Reasonable Faith*, 19.

446. Gould, *Cultural Apologetics*, 13-14.

447. Enfield, *Natural Theology*, iii-iv.

account for the hope that is in you ..." (1 Peter 3:15). Peter clearly desires believers to be prepared to confidently respond to questions from unbelievers. Theistic questions may be included, to which Sudduth asserts, "theistic arguments can rebut or refute atheological objections against theism."[448]

Intellectually-oriented training (at a level common people can comprehend) is required to be prepared with intellectual, philosophical, theistic reasoning. Fulford and Haines argue that "everyone who thinks is doing philosophy ... Christians should learn to philosophize properly ... philosophy is useful to better defend, understand, and articulate Christian doctrines."[449] Gould asserts, "our culture in the West is becoming increasingly post-, sub-, and anti-Christian. ... The problem is not simply 'out there' in culture. The church has grown anti-intellectual and sensate, out of touch with the relevance of Jesus and the gospel to contemporary life. ... the Christian *voice* is muted ... *conscience* is muted ... *imagination* is muted."[450] Gould recommends, "The first step in recovering the Christian intellect ... is gaining an *accurate view of Jesus* ... the authority on all matters of reality. The next step ... is to *view study as part of our apprenticeship to Christ.*"[451]

Intellectual training in theistic and other apologetic reasoning builds confidence for believers to evangelize. Craig observes, "Many Christians do not share their faith with unbelievers simply out of fear. ... nothing inspires confidence and boldness more than knowing that one has good reasons for what one believes and good answers to the typical questions and

---

448. Sudduth, *The Reformed Objection to Natural Theology*, 141.

449. Andrew Fulford and David Haines, "The Metaphysics of Scripture," *Philosophy and the Christian: The Quest for Wisdom in the Light of Christ*, Ed. Joseph Minich (Lincoln, NE: The Davenant Press, 2018), 16-20.

450. Gould, *Cultural Apologetics*, 18-19.

451. Ibid., 172-174.

objections that the unbeliever may raise. Sound training in apologetics is one of the keys to fearless evangelism."[452] Apologetics "equips questioning or doubting Christians to find the intellectual confidence to be wise witnesses to the truth of the gospel," asserts Groothuis, "their knowledge of the truth and rationality for their belief increases, thus giving them a stronger platform for explaining and defending 'the good news.'"[453]

For Scripture Interpretation

Natural theology usage can facilitate proper Scripture interpretation. Paul's clear declaration in Romans 1:18-20 that all men know through general revelation the truth of God (though unbelievers suppress it) implies that what is known through nature (universe and human nature) is a key component of what God expects humans to know through all types of revelation, including special through Scripture. Kemp observes that while Scripture "is the sole infallible source of knowledge," it does not follow that it "is the sole source of *all* knowledge;" therefore, "the arguments that Scripture affirms presume multiple sources of knowledge."[454] Natural theology truths may help us come to more informed interpretations, for "Christians are not immune to making inaccurate conclusions. Thus, we ought to be open to recognizing that our interpretations of some passages of Scriptures could be mistaken," says Jaros, adding, "Sometimes it is our knowledge of natural theology which not only leads us somewhat to the knowledge of God, but may force us to reconsider our interpretations of Scripture."[455]

---

452. Craig, *Reasonable Faith*, 21.

453. Groothuis, *Christian Apologetics* (2011), 41.

454. Kemp, "The Bible, Verification, and First Principles of Reason," 29.

455. Kurt Jaros, "Faith and the Natural Light of Reason," *Without Excuse: Scripture, Reason, and Presuppositional Apologetics*, Ed. David Haines (Leesburg, VA: The Davenant Press, 2020), 52.

An understanding of what nature reveals is central to certain theological understanding. Vos says Scripture assumes natural theology, declaring it "directly [teaches] many things that Scripture does not so much explicitly teach as assume. … to adore the wisdom of God in nature, His ways and His works."[456] Rowland reasons, "consider how the biblical authors write about nature and God's relationship to it and then look at the function of nature and the natural world in the Bible, and their peculiar role in apprehending the divine. This reveals the centrality of nature, in particular human nature, as the key mode of theological understanding."[457] As an example, Koukl argues from nature man's uniqueness from the rest of creation including animals, saying animals have a shallow freedom (rational and willful soul, but not moral) but man a deep freedom (also moral, able to choose based on goodness); therefore, only man can share personal relationship with God.[458] Ross states that ignoring teaching on creation, for example, "obscures foundational Christian doctrines. … the world of nature reveals not only God's existence but also his righteousness and other aspects of his divine nature and attributes," and this ignoring also "discourages systematic theology. The integration of truth … of Scripture with what is revealed in nature's 'book' … is invaluable in developing a consistent and comprehensive theology."[459]

---

456. Vos, *Natural Theology*, 5.

457. Rowland, "Natural Theology and the Christian Bible," 23.

458. Koukl, *The Story of Reality*, 90-91.

459. Ross, *Hidden Treasures in the Book of Job*, 11-12.

Natural theology understandings help to link certain theological themes between multiple Scripture locations. "Natural theology forms an element within scripture and provides important organizing structures within it," according to Barr.[460] He explains,

> principles akin to those of natural theology are present in the Bible ... in certain relations they form the cement which links together various themes of scripture, and equally they form one of the channels through which themes are enabled to pass from the earlier stages of their formulations to the later, most importantly in the connection between Old and New Testaments.[461]

For example, Haines and Fulford ask, "how do we explain the logic of Jesus and Paul, when they declare some parts of the Torah no longer binding on Christians (e.g., Sabbath and Kosher laws), but other parts still in force (e.g., laws against sexual immorality)? Natural law may provide the key here, in that the former examples are clearly 'socially constructed.'"[462]

And going beyond natural theology's impact on certain theological understandings to all understandings, natural theology truths are a precondition to one being able to interpret any Scripture. This follows from Romans 1:18-20 implications, because when general revelation truth is suppressed, one cannot come to faith and be in position to properly interpret. Haines describes the precondition concept, arguing,

> the most basic attempt to interpret Scripture requires, as a precondition, that the interpreter be in possession of a number of important types of natural knowledge: acquired linguistic knowledge, experience and knowledge of the sensible world, philosophical or theoretical knowledge, natural knowledge of the divine nature, and ... hermeneutical principles ... Warfield ... [notes] three major presuppositions ... held by those who engage in ... theology – presuppositions that are established and proved by natural or apologetical theology. ... first ... 'the affirmation that God is, and that He has relation to His creatures.' ... second ... 'the affirmation that man has a religious nature ...

---

460. Barr, *Biblical Faith and Natural Theology*, 198.

461. Ibid., 199.

462. Haines and Fulford, *Natural Law*, 111.

third … 'the affirmation that there are media of communication by which God and divine things are brought before the minds of men …'[463]

Haines points out the example of appropriate predication, saying, "it is natural theology which provides us with the truths necessary for the proper functioning of *the principle of appropriate predication*. This principle … helps the interpreter … know when some attribute is 'properly' predicated of God's divine nature," such as immutability (is) or repentance (is not).[464]

Church Leadership Responsibility

Church leadership holds responsibility for assisting believers with developing their relationship with God, inclusive of natural theology as well as other apologetics. "Church leadership" here primarily means local church pastoral staff, but can include theologians, professors, para-church ministry leaders, etc. Discussion covers current challenges and suggested strategies.

Current challenges to church leadership successfully communicating natural theology and other apologetics to help believers' growth can involve the leaders' expected roles/goals. Moreland proposes,

> how is it possible for a person to be an active member of an evangelical church for twenty or thirty years and still know next to nothing about … the skills and information necessary to preach and defend Christianity in a post-Christian, neo-pagan culture? … *hostility or indifference to the development of an intellectual life in the way we go about our business in the church.* … Forty years ago [the local church pastor] was expected to be a resident authority on theology and biblical teaching. Slowly this gave way to a model of the pastor as the CEO of the church, the administrative and organizational leader. Today the ministers we want are Christianized pop therapists.[465]

---

463. Haines, *Natural Theology*, 21-26.

464. Ibid., 21.

465. J. P. Moreland, *Love Your God with All Your Mind: The Role of Reason in the Life of the Soul*, 2nd Ed. (Colorado Springs, CO: NavPress, Tyndale House, 2012), 219-220.

Certainly, exceptions exist; but generally, the Western Church seems to have become less intellectual and more business and therapy oriented.

Suggested strategies for church leadership successfully communicating natural theology and other apologetics to help believers' growth can involve apologetic training of and cultural engagement by such leaders and ministry inclusive of such knowledge by them to believers. Church leaders without apologetic training need to acquire it. Craig says, "We need … pastors who are schooled in apologetics and engaged intellectually with our culture so as to shepherd their flock amidst the wolves. For example, pastors need to know something about contemporary science … philosophy and biblical criticism … If pastors fail … there will remain a substantial portion of the population … untouched by their ministry."[466]

Regarding ministry inclusive of apologetics to believers, such as services or classes, Chatraw says, "people need others to take their intellectual questions seriously. … … In engaging with objections to the gospel in preaching, we encourage the faith of the faithful and help them deal with their doubts. … The more 'post'-Christian a society becomes, the more we will need to think carefully about our approaches to evangelism, discipleship, and preaching."[467] Chatraw also notes, "If church members know the preacher will respectfully engage their unbelieving friend's secular stories, they are more likely to invite them."[468] Apologetics is also needed for youth, especially those who have unanswered faith questions and could lose their faith, for as Craig observes, "In high school and college Christian teenagers are intellectually assaulted with every manner of non-Christian worldview coupled with an overwhelming

---

466. Craig, *Reasonable Faith*, 20.

467. Chatraw, *Telling a* Better *Story*, 12-13.

468. Ibid., 12-13.

relativism. ... It's insufficient for youth groups and Sunday school classes to focus on entertainment and simpering devotional thoughts. We've got to train our kids for war."[469] Church leadership should plan how to provide adults, university students, and younger youth with apologetics (including natural theology) knowledge, to answer questions and help them engage with culture.

---

469. Craig, *Reasonable Faith*, 19.

CHAPTER 5: CONCLUSION

This chapter concludes the study by providing a summary of its research findings and final recommendations for the Church's natural theology use and further research.

Summary of Research on Natural Theology's Place in the Church

The problem motivating this research is an apparent disparity between the Church's general ignorance of natural theology and both Scripture's reasoning with it and natural theology proponents' reasonable arguments for its use. But what should natural theology's place in the Church be? This study's thesis argues that, although special revelation remains very essential for the Christian life, natural theology is relevant especially in the church ministries of evangelism, impacting culture, and developing believers' relationship with God. That thesis is supported by the previously discussed research findings, which are summarized in this section: from literature review of natural theology, from Scripture review (especially Romans 1:18-20), and from research on relevance of natural theology to church ministries today.

Literature Review Summary

Literature review of natural theology finds that many natural theology proponents exist, though they can have differing views on various points of emphasis and application. This author categorizes the foundational concepts they discuss as: *reason* (the validity of pursuing Christian truth through not only faith but also reason based on reality), *apologetic approaches* (how natural theology reasoning fits within Christian apologetic approaches), *arguments* (its major arguments for Theism), *history* (how its arguments have been used during history), and *today's worldviews* (nontheistic worldviews that Theism defends against).

Natural theology uses *reason* within arguments promoting knowledge of theistic worldview truths. Knowledge of truth, especially that which matters most, should be pursued and must affirm reality. A worldview consists of a set of truths about that which matters most, and should hold up to certain tests, both as individual truths and as a unified set. But how does reason relate to faith? Natural theology proponents assert that reason from general revelation can have value prior to faith in pursuing Christian worldview truth. Moreland and Craig summarize the reason/faith relationship, "In Scripture, faith involves placing trust in what you have reason to believe is true. Faith is not a blind, irrational leap into the dark. So faith and reason cooperate on a biblical view of faith."[470]

Authors commonly categorize major *apologetic approaches* as these four: classical, evidentialist, presuppositionalist, and fideist, with natural theology as an essential subset of classical apologetics. Proponents of nonclassical approaches sometimes incorporate informal natural theology arguments within their materials; more often they do not. Of the four approaches, two emphasize that truth known through reason can lead toward faith: classical and evidentialist. The classical approach reasons both for Theism from natural theology and for Christianity from special revelation, whereas evidentialist reasons solely from historical evidence of special revelation. These two approaches acknowledge that faith can occur without prior conscious reasoning about truth; however, faith commonly follows reason. Further, proponents believe that non-Christians can understand reason about God in spite of the effects of sin. Of the four approaches, the two others emphasize that faith from special revelation is necessary before true reasoning about God occurs: presuppositionalist (faith from Scripture) and fideist (faith from experience).

Natural theology provides reasoned *arguments* for Theism that are commonly categorized into major categories. The four categories are: cosmological (from universe's finite existence),

---

470. Moreland and Craig, *Philosophical Foundations for a Christian Worldview, 2nd Ed.*, 20.

design (i.e., teleological, from universe's designs for life and usefulness), ontological (from human idea of perfect being), and moral (from human conscience's knowing moral absolutes). Other arguments exist from personal human nature beyond the moral argument, including from mind/consciousness, will, beauty recognition, and love. Some authors combine multiple major arguments into a cumulative case argument. Levels of argument scope and formality differ between apologists. Arguments consist of propositions derived from God's general revelation in nature (universe and human nature) and conclusions that the Theistic God exists, sometimes addressing objections such as from naturalism. Conclusions often specify God's attributes, and less often specify humanity's relationship to God.

Natural theology has been used throughout Church *history*. The apologetics of early church fathers includes natural theology, sometimes using arguments promoted by Greek/Roman philosophers. The term "natural theology" is applied as early as Augustine (4th-5th century).[471] In the Late Middle and Renaissance Ages Anselm promotes the ontological argument and Aquinas cosmological arguments. Between Aquinas and the Enlightenment Age's Locke, "a vast change of mentality occurred" in the Church, from natural theology to an evidentialist apologetics focus, according to Wolterstorff.[472] Natural theology was further weakened for many by Darwin's late 1800s naturalistic arguments.[473] Concerning debate of recent centuries about natural theology views of Reformed theologians, Haines concludes that most early reformers believed it valid while various but not all later Reformed theologians believed it invalid.[474]

---

471. Haines, *Natural Theology*, 12.

472. Wolterstorff, "The Migration of the Theistic Arguments," 38, 79.

473. Boa and Bowman, *Faith Has Its Reasons*, 24.

474. Haines, *Natural Theology*, 9.

Today's worldviews can vary widely, but recent apologetic literature focuses on the following:

- Modernism – commonly views objective truth as knowable only by human reason, with no God; sometimes classified by the Naturalism/Matterism (all is matter) derived from it
- Postmodernism – commonly views current truth as socially constructed using human language and objective truth as unknowable or non-existent, with no God
- Monism – commonly views truth as existing within the oneness of everything, which is God, and as revealed in certain circumstances; sometimes classified as Pantheism/Mindism; variants include New Age (every human is God) and Buddhism and some Hindu sects (every human is nothing)
- Theism – views objective truth as revealed by the personal Creator God using general and special revelation which include reason and faith

Most classical apologist authors identify modernism and postmodernism as the two predominant nontheistic worldview classifications of recent centuries, particularly in Western culture. Modernism dominated for centuries, then postmodernism became prominent. Some classical apologists recommend specific natural theology arguments for specific worldviews; many do not. All natural theology arguments might be useful in light of any worldview because no nontheistic worldview acknowledges the personal Creator God. Because individuals' worldviews are unique and few "have well-articulated worldviews,"[475] communication should be unique to the individuals or audience.

Scripture Research Summary

Review of natural theology in Scripture finds that Scripture speaks of things God expects people to observe and reason through general revelation, including acknowledging Him as God and every person accountable to Him. Romans 1:18-20 specifies that this exists, while other

---

475. Groothuis, *Christian Apologetics* (2011), 77.

passages consider various aspects and uses of it. Some passages, such as Romans 1, use natural theology in support of doctrine. Others, such as Acts 14/17, use it within dialogue of believers with unbelievers. Job uses it within dialogue amongst God-fearers and monologue of God to men. When natural theology arguments are made or assumed in Scripture this author considers those passages to contain both general and special revelation, with special confirming the general. Discussion is organized as: exegesis of *Romans 1:18-20*, *Acts 14 and 17* on Paul's gentile apologetic encounters, and *other relevant passages*.

The exegesis of *Romans 1:18-20*, which specifies the critical relationship between God's wrath and human suppression of God's general revelation, suggests potential relevance of natural theology for gospel communication. Paul summarizes the human unrighteousness problem with God: although God has revealed through nature sufficient knowledge of Himself and His expectations for humans to live righteously, humans have chosen to suppress that knowledge and live in ungodliness and unrighteousness, thus invoking His wrath. Some natural theology objectors argue from a perspective of sin's overwhelming noetic effects on human reason to condemn natural theology. But Paul's terminology is quite clear that unbelievers truly have sufficient knowledge of God though they suppress it; thus, they are condemned by it. If unbelievers are not responsive to solely special revelation arguments about salvation through righteousness by faith in Christ's works, then natural theology arguments are valid potential tools to help them first un-suppress the truth of the Theistic God and accountability to Him.

Acts 14 and 17 record dialogue by Paul using natural theology arguments which are consistent with Romans 1:18-20's accountability of man to God. When addressing unbelieving Jews or gentiles judging his Judaism, Paul references Scripture and/or Christ's works. By contrast, in Acts 14 and 17, when addressing gentiles not judging his Judaism and having no basic Scripture knowledge, Paul begins at a more foundational level, with natural theology, for "pagans must first be taught what Jews already confess regarding the unity and character of God."[476] In chapters 14 and 17 Paul argues similarly that nature reveals one living God who is Creator, Ruler, and Provider and is to be worshipped.

Other relevant passages beyond Romans 1 and Acts 14/17 use natural theology arguments which are consistent with Romans 1:18-20's accountability of man to God. Some reference natural theology argumentation directly, asking the audience to reason clear conclusions from nature, while others reference it indirectly, assuming the audience should be aware of certain conclusions. The Book of Job contains natural theology arguments made both by men to each other and by God to Job. Job chapters 3-37 reveal the firm belief in general revelation by the five men discussing Job's suffering. Chapters 38-42 reveal God speaking lessons to Job from nature (which might be considered both general and special revelation). Additional Scripture passages (including Psalms 19, 8, 104, Matt. 6) either point out that God "speaks" through the universe or asks the audience to observe it and reason important conclusions about God and/or man. God's universe "speech" comes through nature (the physical and life forms with soul/spirit) and through history. Further passages indicate that God "speaks" through personal aspects of human nature in ways that should cause all to draw the same conclusions about God and man. God's human nature "speech" comes through awareness and use of God-given human capacities such as morality (good vs. evil; from Psalm 19, 119, "natural" things passages), wisdom (wise vs. foolish; from Proverbs, Matt. 18), and reason.

---

476. Haines, *Natural Theology*, quoting Bruce, 30-31.

Relevance to Church Ministries Today Summary

Research on the relevance of natural theology today finds that it might be utilized within three primary church ministries to help un-suppress theistic truth: *evangelism, impacting culture,* and *developing believers' relationship with God*. Use of natural theology by these ministries may seem challenging because clear reasoning is needed. But natural theology use does not necessarily involve presenting formal philosophical proofs with lengthy proposition and conclusion statements, though it can. Rather, arguments should be communicated in manners amenable to the circumstance and audience, whether the learned and/or unlearned.

In the Church's *evangelism* ministry, natural theology utilization may help unbelievers to understand Christianity's theistic basis and how their own worldviews have deficiencies, with believers considering at least the following: being personal, as in all apologetics; finding common ground for theistic discussion; and reasoning theistic truths in contrast with nontheistic beliefs. Multiple authors reference Schaeffer's assertion that Christianity does not start with Jesus saves from sins but rather from in the beginning God created. Classical apologetics is consistent with this, having two parts with the first reasoning theism and the second Christianity's salvation. If the second part is used first and unsuccessfully, one might need to use the first part to address nontheistic worldview beliefs. Being personal includes seeking to understand people's assumptions and meanings of terms. Finding common ground involves exploring beliefs that unbelievers already possess that are in common with theism. Craig observes, "No atheist or agnostic really lives consistently with his worldview. In some way he affirms meaning, value, or purpose without an adequate basis. ... the Christian has a foundation ... for the values he already possesses."[477] If an unbeliever seems to reject the notion of

---

477. Craig, *Reasonable Faith*, 86-87.

knowable objective spiritual truth, as can be true of postmodernists, then the nature of such truth should be discussed. With an unbeliever's primary nontheistic beliefs and their logical conclusions identified, evangelistic discussion should show how contrasting theistic truths provide an internally consistent and livable worldview. Modernists might be more concerned with consistency, postmodernists and monists possibly with livability.

In the Church's ministry of *impacting culture*, natural theology utilization may be helpful in at least two ways: impacting collective cultural thought toward accepting that the gospel's theistic foundation is based on reason and impacting specific cultural spheres toward increased truth and resulting good. Culture's collective thought (current narrative's primary ideas) sometimes accepts theistic truths but more often denies them. The Church should use natural theology to impact culture's collective thought, not solely for the sake of theism's prominence, but for the sake of the gospel having greater opportunity due to its theistic foundation being rejected less frequently. Craig declares "it is the broader task of Christian apologetics to help create and sustain a cultural milieu in which the gospel can be heard as an intellectually viable option for thinking men and women."[478] Natural theology truths communicated within specific cultural spheres can also increase the truth and resulting good in those spheres. Today's cultural sphere of science/technology needs natural theology's influence, especially because in that sphere people are "deeply modernist."[479] We "should seek to show that Christianity is consistent with the scientific facts," while being cautious about the latest theories posed by scientists.[480] Today's sphere of education (university and primary/secondary), which impacts a person's

---

478. Ibid., 16-19.

479. Ibid.

480. Boa and Bowman, *Faith Has Its Reasons*, 80.

worldview for their lifetime, needs natural theology's influence from the Church. The government/law sphere also needs natural theology influence. When government officials at any level do not operate according to a standard of good for all, which the moral argument promotes, injustice to someone results. The Church should not seek to rule over government/law, but should impact it by communicating natural theology truths as needed to encourage it to serve people's good.

In the Church's ministry of *developing believers' relationship with God*, commonly termed discipleship, natural theology utilization may be helpful. Natural theology as well as evidentialist arguments focus on the mind/intellect; both heart and mind growth are important to a relationship with God. Generally, natural theology use in discipleship should strengthen the theistic beliefs of the believer, including providing a broader picture of the full set of Christian beliefs. Concerning knowing God better, natural theology helps believers know more of God and thus be more satisfied in their faith. Concerning resolving doubts, apologetic reasoning (including natural theology) "fortifies believers in their faith, whether they are wrestling with doubts and questions or simply seeking a deeper grounding for their biblical beliefs."[481] Concerning persevering, apologetics use to help believers to know God better and resolve intellectual doubts can reduce apostasy. Natural theology can facilitate a believer's confident preparation for evangelism and cultural impact. From apologetics training, a believer's "knowledge of the truth and rationality for their belief increases, thus giving them a stronger platform for explaining and defending 'the good news.'"[482] Natural theology usage can facilitate proper Scripture interpretation. Kemp observes that while Scripture "is the sole infallible source

---

481. Groothuis, *Christian Apologetics* (2011), 25.

482. Ibid., 41.

of knowledge," it is not "the sole source of *all* knowledge."[483] An understanding of what nature reveals is central to certain theological understanding. Vos says Scripture assumes natural theology, declaring it "directly [teaches] many things that Scripture does not so much explicitly teach as assume."[484] Natural theology understandings help to link certain theological themes between multiple Scripture locations. And natural theology truths are a precondition to one being able to correctly interpret Scripture. Church leadership holds responsibility for assisting believers with developing their relationship with God, inclusive of natural theology as well as other apologetics. Current challenges to church leadership undertaking this can involve the leaders' primary expected roles/goals being other than theologian and Bible teacher. Suggested strategies for church leadership include participating in apologetic training, engaging cultural issues themselves, and providing apologetic ministry and training to adults and youth, whether in services/classes or individually.

Final Recommendations on Natural Theology Use and Further Research

This section provides final recommendations regarding natural theology – on its use and on further research.

Recommendations for Use Today

Haines summarizes well, saying, "God reveals Himself to us in his world (in each of its elements: the natural world, human history, and even the individual human being), in His Word, and in His Church," and further clarifying God's world revelation,

> Through His world He reveals Himself as great and majestic, distinct, beyond our imagination and even our words, ineffable, immutable, eternal, omnipotent, … Good, True, and Beautiful; but also as worthy of worship and as the judge of those who turn from Him to idolatry and evil. We are all prone to turn from God. To those who will

---

483. Kemp, "The Bible, Verification, and First Principles of Reason," 29.

484. Vos, *Natural Theology*, 5.

listen, this world calls us back. We are all prone to ... 'practical atheism.' Natural theology ... is a great remedy for this spiritual sickness.[485]

Natural theology provides not only a set of philosophical arguments for Christianity's theistic foundation, but also a tool for the Church. Its arguments (not including ontological) might be summarized as:

- **Universe** – Reasoning from observation of the universe's existence/sustenance and its complex order, including absolute truths and provision for life, concludes existence of a God with theistic attributes as its cause and designer and accountability of man to Him.
- **Human Nature** – Reasoning from observation of human nature's existence and freedom in greatness and lowliness, including its immaterial features of rational mind, moral conscience, intentional will, perception of beauty, etc., concludes existence of a God with theistic attributes as personal creator and accountability of man to Him.

Church leaders and individuals should make use of natural theology arguments in various ways. Note that the term church leaders includes not only the primary local church leader/pastor but also other local church leaders and leaders of other types of ministry organizations/groups. Chapter 4 (Natural Theology's Relevance Today) and its summary in a prior Chapter 5 subsection (Relevance to Church Ministries Today Summary) discuss how natural theology could be used in the church ministries of evangelism, impacting culture, and developing believers' relationship with God. Key actions for consideration by *church leaders* and *individual believers* follow.

Church leaders are responsible before God for themselves and those they serve, and therefore first must determine whether natural theology has validity. If so, and if they are not promoting its use, they should first consider obtaining training in it (whether classes, mentoring, or personal research). Then, they should personally engage culture with it; that is, consider cultural issues through the lens of worldview beliefs and their relationship to Theism. Then,

---

485. Haines, *Natural Theology*, v.

consider whether and how to minister using it and how to train believers in it. That ministry/training should be provided both for general development of the believers' relationship with God (which includes how they impact culture using it) and for evangelism use specifically (with greater detail on how to apply it.).

Individual believers should respond similarly. They are responsible before God for themselves, and therefore first must determine whether natural theology has validity. If so, and if they are not using it, they should first consider obtaining training in it (whether classes, mentoring, or personal research). Then, they should personally engage culture with it; that is, consider cultural issues through the lens of worldview beliefs and their relationship to Theism. Then, consider whether and how to communicate with others using it, including in evangelism, impacting culture, interacting with other believers to encourage them. One might also assist local church leadership in promoting its use and training for it.

Recommendations for Further Research

The following recommendations result from this author's research not encountering, or not encountering sufficiently in an accessible and organized manner, certain material that could facilitate natural theology practical application in evangelism, impacting culture, and developing believers' relationship with God. This research includes providing: clear argument versions, identification of man's accountability within arguments, Scripture support for arguments, argument connections with evidentialist arguments, argument correlation to nontheistic worldview beliefs, cultural spheres application, and classical apologetics materials availability.

Clear Argument Versions: Research should provide one simplified and one complex logical argument version for each natural argument category. The same should be provided for the cumulative case argument (after work on others). The simplified versions would be most beneficial for the lesser philosophically oriented believer and the complex versions for the more philosophically oriented. The complex versions should include multiple sub-arguments within (as needed) and rebuttals of major objections. These versions could be helpful because, though many authors make important contributions to an argument category, few provide clear summary versions of the complete argument in forms that much of the Church can learn and use.

Identification of Man's Accountability within Arguments: Research should enhance the complex version (and simplified if applicable) of each natural argument category to clearly identify man's accountability to and failures before God (which leads to the need for Christ's gospel but does not resolve it). This accountability may be quite general for the cosmological argument, but more specific for others (for example, teleological – not using things for intentional good based on their design). This may be helpful because many presentations of specific arguments do not clearly identify man's accountability.

Scripture Support for Arguments: Research should provide key Scripture passages (with analysis) that support each natural theology argument category. This could be helpful not only to boost believers' confidence in the argument's basis, but to assist those currently promoting non-classical apologetic approaches to consider incorporation of natural theology arguments.

Argument Connections with Evidentialist Arguments: Research should identify whether connections exist between specific natural theology arguments and common evidentialist arguments. Natural theology literature does not seem to address this specifically, rather it portrays each as separate classical apologetics steps without connecting them other than the one concluding accountability to and failure before God and the other solving that dilemma.

Argument Correlation to Nontheistic Worldview Beliefs: Research should provide clear correlation of specific natural theology arguments to specific nontheistic worldview beliefs.

Some authors discuss approaches to worldviews but few delineate specific recommendations correlating arguments to specific beliefs.

Argument Application to Cultural Spheres: Research should provide application of specific natural theology arguments to the various cultural spheres (as those in prior discussions on impacting culture). Some authors discuss such application (which may seem obvious to some), but many only note the need to impact the spheres.

Classical Apologetic Materials Availability: Research should provide a summary and analysis of currently available and up-to-date training materials on classical apologetics, in formats for the Church's use in training believers generally and for evangelism specifically.

www.ingramcontent.com/pod-product-compliance
Lightning Source LLC
Chambersburg PA
CBHW052148110526
44591CB00012B/1899